Modern-day Miracles

from the
Files of President Harold B. Lee

Selected, Arranged, and Edited by
L. Brent Goates

Published by Covenant Communications, Inc.
American Fork, Utah

Printed in the United States of America
First Printing: March 1996

01 00 99 98 97 96   10 9 8 7 6 5 4 3 2

ISBN 1-55503-915-4

"This is a day of miracles. They are happening among us all the time, if we only live in such a way that God can use us as his instruments by which these miraculous things can be done. I say to you the day of miracles has not passed."

—President Harold B. Lee

Table of Contents

Preface

There is a power beyond the sight of man that heals not only sick bodies but sick souls.... Yes, the Lord can heal sick bodies, but the greatest miracles we see are the healing of sick souls.

President Harold B. Lee[1] made this statement in his Baccalaureate Address at Ricks College on May 6, 1970. When a former seminary student described to him the gradual conversion of her husband, President Lee wrote to her:

[That] is a testimony of real merit. I have in my desk a file with the tab marked "Modern Miracles." To me, the healing of a sick soul is as great as the healing of a sick body.

After President Lee's death, the file to which he made reference was found. It contained over sixty separate miracle stories, most of them describing the healing of sick bodies, all of them telling of lives changed for the better.

President Lee was an instinctive, inveterate believer in miracles. He was quietly but keenly interested in them and maintained his file as a verification of his faith in modern-day miracles. When people wrote to him of miraculous results from his labors amongst the Saints, he often wrote back to them to document the event and circumstances. These letters he would place in his "Miracle File" as one more demonstration of God's goodness in rewarding faith.

President Lee was always a believer in miracles, although early in his mature life he was more careful in choosing those with whom he would share them. When he first entered into the Quorum of the Twelve Apostles in 1941, he privately wrote in his journal expressing his disappointment that even in that select circle he felt constrained in reporting the miraculous because of the attitudes of some of his brethren.

An incident in 1954 illustrates a true Harold B. Lee characteristic: he always sought first the miracle and believed with a pure heart, never doubting. He rarely quoted from his miracle file but he did so on two occasions when speaking to seminary leaders assembled on the BYU campus in 1969 and 1970. He related this story:

I came on this campus in 1954 each day for five or six weeks for a class with all the seminary and some of the institute teachers. It was a grueling summer, but I learned, along with them. We had a glorious time together.

At the conclusion we had a banquet, something like the one we had tonight, only President [J. Reuben] Clark and Brother [Henry D.] Moyle had come down to be with us. We were seated at the front and the tables before us were fixed so that all of them could get a side view of the speaker's stand. At the conclusion of the banquet one of these seminary teachers took me aside. He came with glistening tears in his eyes and was almost trembling as he said:

"Come over here in this corner, Brother Lee. I have got to tell you something. My wife and I were sitting over there at that table. We were looking over into this corner. Suddenly there appeared the faces of the Prophet Joseph Smith and Brigham Young. I thought, Isn't that marvelous to see the pictures of these two men together? As I watched, that picture faded; it wasn't there anymore. I turned to my wife and said, "Did you see that picture?" She replied, "I didn't see anything." But even though there is no picture there now, Brother Lee, it was there. I saw it: I wasn't dreaming!

"I'm not surprised," I said. "Aren't you aware of the fact that all through our summer course we have been quoting from the words of the Prophet Joseph Smith and President Brigham Young? Why wouldn't they want to be here? Where else would they rather be on such an occasion than to be permitted to come here at the conclusion of this great seminar where you are going out to influence 150,000 youth from all over this Church? I wouldn't be surprised that they are very close, to let their spirits attend such a gathering. Perhaps most haven't seen them, but have no doubt that they were here. Heaven isn't a million miles away. It's here."

President Lee was always willing to cheerfully share his immense spiritual gifts with others; he bore the burden of frequently giving priesthood blessings to his brethren, his family, his friends, to anyone in need. His attitude of service is reflected in this brief reference made by President Thomas S. Monson recalling a personal experience with President Lee:

> In a more solemn setting, Brother Lee met me one evening on the steps of the LDS Hospital in Salt Lake City. By appointment we were to give a blessing to my eldest son, Tom, who was then in his later teens. Surgery awaited which could be of a most serious nature. Brother Lee took my hand before we ascended the stairs and, looking me straight in the eye, said, "Tom, there is no place I would rather be at this moment than by your side to participate with you in providing a sacred priesthood blessing to your son."[2]

Modern-day miracles are not confined to General Authorities of the Church. Almost every faithful family has its own treasured miracle file. As did President Lee, many people record and cherish these stories as instruments to build faith among family members. All Saints are commanded to pray and exercise faith. In some cases miracles result; other times answers come in different ways, and sometimes, the response is negative, as when Elder Lee was asked to give a healing blessing to a friend of his. He said, "The Lord has other plans, and he determines not only what we promise but what will happen."

For reasons that no doubt are good and sufficient, because they are His, the Lord has commanded that we acknowledge His hand in all things. But He did want us to be humble, to be grateful for His blessings, and to be constantly reminded to live the eternal laws upon which His blessings are predicated.

One grateful recipient of a miracle, Richard W. Madsen III, ponders the need for miracles in our lives:

> [Probably] the Lord knew that some persons are dependent upon the testimony of divine manifestations in mortal lives to accept the unseen and to bolster quavering faith. Not all can rationalize an understanding of eternal actuality, nor be gifted with the testimony of the Spirit. Some need the crutch of reassurances from others who have been blessed with extraordinary experiences.

Early in the process of compiling these stories, I became curious (as surely readers must) about the staying power of the miracles in the lives of the beneficiaries. To satisfy these questions, I made attempts to locate the individuals in the stories, a task not easy after thirty, forty, and even fifty years have passed since the hand of God had moved upon them. This has led to a fascinating study of courage to maintain belief amidst the constant pounding of the adversities of life and the onslaught of Satan to destroy faith. The updated commentaries from these people have sometimes uncovered even greater miracles and explanations, but they have never failed to add interest to this study of the striving of the soul for spiritual victory.

May the blessing of faith, which prompted President Lee to compile his treasured trove of inspiring stories, now come upon all readers of this book, that we may rejoice together in the generosity of our Father in providing so many wonderful "modern-day miracles."

L. Brent Goates

Notes

[1]President Lee is alternately referred to as Brother Lee, Elder Lee, and President Lee, according to his calling at the time of the incident referred to.

[2]From the General Priesthood Session of the 164th Annual General Conference of the Church, 2 April 1994 (*Ensign*, May 1994, p. 51).

Introduction

Every time I see a newborn baby cry, or touch a leaf, or see the sky, then I know why, I believe ...[1]

A flaming sunset ... a sleeping baby ... a soaring hawk ... Miracles like these have moved us with reverence and awe. Through such experiences we see the world around us with new eyes and broader, deeper understanding.

But miracles of the Biblical variety haven't carried much credibility in recent centuries, at least not the magnitude of miracles with lasting impact, such as the parting of the Red Sea.

But suppose one such miracle did happen in this age of high science and technology. In days long past, people would have dropped to their knees in awe. Today most of us probably would rush to the scientist at the nearest university for confirmation that we had, in fact, witnessed an example of divine intervention. And that could be the first sign of our own flagging faith.

All this was predicted by latter-day revelation. The Book of Mormon foretells its own emergence in these words:

> And no one need say they shall not come, for they surely shall, for the Lord hath spoken it; for out of the earth shall they come, by the hand of the Lord, and none can stay it; and it shall come in a day when it shall be said that miracles are done away; and it shall come even as if one should speak from the dead. (Mormon 8:26)

> And it shall come to pass ... the Gentiles are lifted up in the pride of their eyes, and have stumbled ... that they have built up many churches; nevertheless they put down the power and miracles of God, and preach up unto themselves their own

wisdom and their own learning, that they may get gain and grind upon the face of the poor. (2 Nephi 26:19-20)

When the Savior organized the kingdom of God during His days on earth He called twelve apostles and endowed them with spiritual gifts and said to His beloved leaders:

> And these signs shall follow them that believe; In my name shall they cast out devils; they shall speak with new tongues; They shall take up serpents; and if they drink any deadly thing, it shall not hurt them: they shall lay hands on the sick, and they shall recover. (Mark 16:17-18)

In 1 Corinthians chapter 12, the Apostle Paul provides a more comprehensive explanation of spiritual gifts in that day.

When the gospel was restored in the dispensation of the fullness of times, the same recital of spiritual gifts is enumerated (see D&C 46:10-29). The consistency in these teachings demonstrates that the restoration of the gospel through the Prophet Joseph Smith did, in fact, bring back to the earth the same Church organization, possessing the same spiritual gifts and powers that existed in the primitive Church.

Wherever the Kingdom of God is organized upon the earth one should expect to find miracles performed among the Saints.

Definition of Miracles

What precisely do we mean when we speak of a miracle? To most of us, a miracle relates to some effect in the physical world that surpasses all known human or natural powers and is therefore ascribed to supernatural agencies. Scientists would have no explanation of such inexplicable and irreproducible phenomena as miracles. *Webster's Third New International Dictionary* (1971) gives these definitions:

a. "an extraordinary event, taken to manifest the supernatural power of God fulfilling His purposes (perform the healings described in the Gospels)."

1b. "an event or effect in the physical world deviating from the laws of nature."

2a. "an accomplishment or occurrence so outstanding or unusual as to seem beyond human capability."

2b. "a wonderful thing worthy of admiration; a truly superb representative of its kind."

Not all miracles, therefore, would apply to time, space, and physical objects. Definitions 2a and 2b even allow for the common usage in English of the word "miracle" to cover such situations as an amazing escape unharmed from a devestating automobile or airplane crash.

The sporting world has its miracles, too, such as the baseball no-hit game that stands out from all others because it was pitched in September 1993 by Jim Abbott of the New York Yankees, the only one-handed pitcher to play the game.

A week later at the U. S. Open Tennis Tournament in New York there was a miraculous rally by Australia's Wally Masur, who fought back after losing the first two sets, only to trail 0-5 in the fifth set, to amazingly earn a 7-5 victory in the last set over countryman Jamie Morgan. After fighting off a match point in the seventh game of the fifth set, Masur, 30, won 16 straight points and 18 of the final 19, in one of the greatest comeback performances in tennis history.

Parting the Red Sea

And Moses stretched out his hand over the sea; and the Lord caused the sea to go back by a strong east wind all that night, and made the sea dry land, and the waters were divided.

And the children of Israel went into the midst of the sea upon the dry ground. (Exodus 14:21-22)

This spectacular moment almost has no equal in Biblical lore and has earned universal recognition as a king-sized miracle. Although familiar to most everyone it has taken great faith to believe in the Biblical text. Yet, recently, in a rare moment of support, some scientists have proffered an explanation for this amazing phenomena.

Sophisticated computer calculations indicate that the Biblical parting of the Red Sea, which allowed Moses and the Israelites to escape from bondage in Egypt, could have occurred precisely as the Bible describes it. A report in the *Bulletin of the American Meteorological Society* in 1992 states that because of the peculiar geography of the northern end of the Red Sea, a moderate wind blowing constantly for about ten hours could have caused the sea to recede about a mile, and have the water level drop ten feet.[2] This would leave dry land in the area where many Biblical scholars believe the crossing occurred.

An abrupt change in the wind would have then allowed the waters to come crashing back into the area in a few brief moments, a phenomenon that the Bible says inundated the Israelites' pursuers.

Most scholars agree that the Israelites did not cross the Red Sea itself, but the Gulf of Suez, which is a northern extension of the sea. The crossing probably occurred at the northern end of the gulf, around the site of the modern town of Suez.

Oceanographer Gabriel Csanady of Old Dominion University in Norfolk, Conn., told the *Los Angeles Times* that the new scenario was "very plausible."[3]

Meteorologist Nathan Paldor, who was on sabbatical at the University of Rhode Island from Hebrew University of Jerusalem, said he became interested in the problem because of his acquaintance with the Biblical descriptions and because it is an "interesting, unsolved problem in physical oceanography. The problem consists of simple physical laws—which are well-known—and a complicated set of equations that describe what happens to the water when the wind acts on it."[4]

The great Creator of the universe, we could assume, would use His omniscience to perform what we call miracles, perhaps by simply utilizing the laws of physics in a manner mortal man is slowly learning.

Other Old Testament Miracles

Two scriptural situations, generally considered so fantastic as to be ridiculous to the unbelieving mind, are recorded in Joshua 10:8-14 and 2 Kings 20:1-11.

Joshua asked the Lord to make the sun stand still, and the moon stayed, too. The Prophet Isaiah, in predicting the death of King Hezekiah, spoke to the Lord, who brought the sun backwards ten degrees.

With reference to these most difficult-to-believe Biblical miracles, Mr. Harold Hill, president of the Curtis Engine Company in Baltimore, Maryland, a consultant in the U. S. space program, stated in an article published in April 1972, that modern technology has enabled space scientists to look back and account for such solar deviations.[5] If true, it is another rare instance where science may be lending a helping hand to faith to believe in miracles.

Water Converted into Wine

The first miracle of Jesus recorded in the New Testament (John 2:1-11) was the conversion of water into wine at a wedding feast. This occurred in Cana of Galilee in March, A.D. 27. Tourists today still find this single event to be the sole reason to visit this tiny village in Israel.

Jesus and his disciples were invited to attend the wedding where, apparently, Mary, the mother of Jesus, was providing some hospitality. Perhaps it was a family marriage for a relative of Jesus. At some point in time the mother of Jesus informed Him of a lack of wine. Mary then instructed the servants to do whatsoever Jesus asked, apparently fully confident that He would solve the shortage problem. Only theories are offered as to the purpose of performing this miracle.

The Savior instructed that six waterpots of stone, containing two or three "firkins" apiece, be filled with water to the brim. This would contain from 120 to 180 gallons, according to some scholars.

It seems that the miraculous change of the liquid in the containers occurred almost instantaneously since Jesus asks, in the next verse, that the new wine be carried to the governor of the feast. The quality of the wine was so impressive that the governor observed they had "kept the good wine until now." He didn't know the origin of the "good" wine, but "the servants which drew the water knew."

The Joseph Smith Translation (Inspired Version) adds little, except to show a much more intimate relationship between Jesus and His mother. In John 2:4 the dialogue appears more harsh: "Woman, what have I to do with thee? mine hour is not yet come." In the Joseph Smith Translation, it is rendered: "Woman, what wilt thou have me to do for thee? That will I do, for mine hour is not yet come."

At least one benefit is found in the reaction of His disciples in beholding their first miracle. The Biblical text is changed from "and his disciples *believed on him*" to read "and *the faith* of His disciples was *strengthened in Him.*"

Joseph Smith's First Miracle

The "discerning of spirits" and the "working of miracles" are specifically mentioned as gifts of the spirit by the Apostle Paul and the Lord in the Doctrine and Covenants section 64, and "in my name shall they cast out devils" was included in the original pronouncement by the Savior (Mark 16:17). It was this gift of the Spirit that was to first introduce the power to perform miracles in the newly restored Church.

Only a few weeks after the organization of the Church in April 1830, the Prophet Joseph Smith went on a visit to see the Joseph Knight family in Colesville, Broome County, New York. While

there, he had many serious discussions on religion with Newel
Knight, son of Joseph Knight. The Prophet urged Newel to pray
vocally at their meetings, but he declined. Later, Newell felt so
badly about refusing to pray he went into the woods to pray in
private, but found that impossible also. When he returned to his
own house his appearance was so alarming that his wife was
frightened and sent for Joseph, the Prophet, to come to their aid.
Joseph writes of this incident in his *History of the Church:*

> I went and found him suffering very much in his mind,
> and his body acted upon in a very strange manner; his visage
> and limbs distorted and twisted in every shape and appearance
> possible to imagine; and finally he was caught up off the floor
> of the apartment, and tossed about most fearfully.
>
> His situation was soon made known to his neighbors and
> relatives, and in a short time as many as eight or nine grown
> persons had got together to witness the scene. After he had
> thus suffered for a time, I succeeded in getting hold of him by
> the hand, when almost immediately he spoke to me, and with
> great earnestness requested me to cast the devil out of him, say-
> ing that he knew he was in him and that he also knew that I
> could cast him out.
>
> I replied, "If you know that I can, it shall be done;" and
> then almost unconsciously I rebuked the devil, and com-
> manded him in the name of Jesus Christ to depart from him;
> when immediately Newel spoke out and said that he saw the
> devil leave him and vanish from his sight.
>
> This was the first miracle which was done in the Church,
> or by any member of it; and it was done not by man, nor the
> power of man, but it was done by God, and by the power of
> godliness; therefore, let the honor and the praise, the domin-
> ion and the glory, be ascribed to the Father, Son and Holy
> Spirit, for ever and ever. Amen. (*HC* 1:83)

A complete change came over Newel Knight after this experience. His countenance became natural, his distortions of body ceased and almost immediately the visions of eternity were opened to his view. After resting for some time Newel related his spiritual manifestation as follows:

> I now began to feel a most pleasing sensation resting on me, and immediately the visions of heaven were opened to my view. I felt myself attracted upward, and remained for some time enwrapt in contemplation, insomuch that I knew not what was going on in the room. By and by, I felt some weight pressing upon my shoulder and the side of my head, which served to recall me to a sense of my situation, and I found that the Spirit of the Lord had actually caught me up off the floor, and that my shoulder and head were pressing against the beams.

Many persons witnessed this first miracle to their great amazement. The casting off of an evil spirit and the power of God made manifest thereafter combined to make believers of many future converts to the Church. One month later Newel Knight came to Fayette and was baptized by David Whitmer.

Healing of the Sick

Of the nine or ten spiritual gifts always listed in modern scripture (see Moroni 10:17 and D&C 46:11-29), none seem to be more commonplace among us than the gift of healing the sick.

Human suffering is a part of mortal life and has been as far back as we know of the life of man. The multiplicity of disease attacks and accidental injuries bring to us and our friends an ever constant recurrence of physical and mental distress.

Our understanding of the gospel teaches us that this is part of the plan of life designed for man. Adam and Eve were driven out of the Garden of Eden intentionally so that they could meet the opposing elements of adverse mortal life. This was essential in the great divine plan.

The grand design provided also for the final death of man. It was planned that the destroying forces of nature—by us called disease, accident, or deterioration of the body or mind—should at some time terminate his mortal career.

To counteract, in part, these destructive forces, God placed at the disposal of man healing herbs, antidotes, and various medicines; He also gave men the intelligence with which to use these aids. Transcending all of these, God stands ready to interpose with His own miraculous power in behalf of those who are worthy and have faith in Him.

In Biblical days the Apostle James outlined the procedure for healing the sick. He instructed:

> Is any sick among you? Let him call for the elders of the Church; and let them pray over him, anointing him with oil in the name of the Lord; and the prayer of faith shall save the sick, and the Lord shall raise him up; and if he have committed sins, they shall be forgiven him. (James 5:14-15)

The procedure is remarkably the same today and is a common occurrence in The Church of Jesus Christ of Latter-day Saints. It is known as administering to the sick. It is done as a function of the holy priesthood—the power by which the sick were healed in the meridian of time; the power by which the Earth was made and by which all the organization of God's kingdom functions.

It is important to understand that not always do the prayers of faith or administrations of the priesthood save the sick. It is appointed unto man sometime to die. When his course is run, when his work is finished, when God calls him home, neither the prayers of the faithful nor the power of the priesthood may interfere. Neither should we want them to do so.

We should exercise our faith in *the healing ordinances of the Church* knowing that God will give full recognition to them, but let us always be willing to say: "Thy will, not mine, be done." In our dispensation the Lord has given us this instruction with a promise:

And whosoever among you are sick, and have not faith to be healed, but believe, shall be nourished with all tenderness, with herbs and mild food, and that not by the hand of an enemy.

And the elders of the Church, two or more, shall be called, and shall pray for and lay their hands upon them in my name; and if they die they shall die unto me, and if they live they shall live unto me.

Thou shalt live together in love, insomuch that thou shall weep for the loss of them that die, and more especially for those that have not hope of a glorious resurrection.

And it shall come to pass that those that die in me shall not taste of death, for it shall be sweet unto them;

And they that die not in me, wo unto them, for their death is bitter.

And again, it shall come to pass that he that hath faith in me to be healed, and is not *appointed unto death*, shall be healed.

He who hath faith to see shall see.

He who hath faith to hear shall hear.

The lame who hath faith to leap shall leap. (D&C 42:43-51; emphasis added)

President Harold B. Lee's "miracle file" contained letters from individuals whose lives had been touched by miracles. One young college coed wrote later, "To have an apostle put his arms around you and cradle you like a little child and bless you was like nothing I could imagine. I got a glimpse of Christlike love...."

Sonya Watts Burnidge described the unforgettable vision she had at age 17 when she saw the Savior standing near to Elder Lee who as an apostle was speaking at a stake conference in Idaho. She wrote to Elder Lee, describing her experience, and received the following reply:

Undoubtedly such as you saw was given to you because of your worthiness and preparation for it. If you will guard it sacredly and continue to live worthily, the Lord will continue to bless you with the inspiration of his Holy Spirit.

One man told how he had attended conference and "prayed that someone would tell me how to repent. As [Elder Lee] stood and addressed the audience, [he] stated, 'I won't give my prepared talk today because someone here wants to know how to repent.'"

Countless stories were related by grateful mothers who had sought a maternity blessing at Elder Lee's hands and were later able to bear children. Over a dozen named their sons after him. Some women were additionally able to adopt children as well.

Of course, the reports from President Harold B. Lee's "miracle file" found in the pages of this book are only a few of the many instances where healings have been experienced by the Saints throughout the Church in our day. Miraculous healings take place daily, and yet they are often suppressed. While many are no doubt reserved to keep the stories private and sacred, this practice of suppression can make our people wonder if miracles are still with us as God's chosen ones.

Wherever the true church of God exists, there will be found this gift of divine healing as one of the signs that follow the believer. We should be careful to note, however, that it is not an exclusive distinguishing sign, for many spiritual healings are found outside of the true Church and even beyond what might be called orthodox Christianity.

The presence of healings and miracles amongst us is a barometer of sorts by which we may gauge the level of our faith and our acceptance by God. This is made clear from the scriptures:

And if there were miracles wrought [by Christ] then, why has God ceased to be a God of miracles and yet be an unchangeable Being? And behold, I say unto you he changeth not; if so he would cease to be God; and he ceaseth not to be

God, and is a God of miracles.

And the reason why he ceaseth to do miracles among the children of men is because that they dwindle in unbelief, and depart from the right way, and know not the God in whom they should trust. (Mormon 9:19-20)

For behold, I am God; and I am a God of miracles; and I will show unto the world that I am the same yesterday, today, and forever; and I work not among the children of men save it be according to their faith. (2 Nephi 27:23)

Our faith determines the miracle, as the Savior himself explained by comparing His own ministrations on two continents:

So great faith have I never seen among all the Jews; wherefore I could not show unto them so great miracles, because of their unbelief.

Verily I say unto you, there are none of them that have seen so great things as ye have seen; neither have they heard so great things as ye have heard. (3 Nephi 19:35-36)

Other qualitative differences may depend upon whether the Priesthood officiator has the "gifts of healing" (Moroni 10:11) and the recipient of the blessing has "the faith to be healed" (D&C 46:19).

And now I speak unto all the ends of the earth—that if the day cometh that the power and gifts of God shall be done away among you, it shall be because of unbelief." (Moroni 10:24)

We should conscientiously strive to build our faith and seek after and cultivate the gifts of the Spirit promised to the Saints. To do so is to demonstrate anew that God is a God of miracles, and that *we are a people approved of God because He honors our righteous supplications with miracles. Humbly we can certify our-*

selves as His Church and people by announcing that miracles still flow through this Kingdom of God on Earth, for "these signs shall follow those that believe, in my name" (Mark 16:16).

Let us have as our slogan "Expect A Miracle," and then give praise to God as we gratefully acknowledge His generous and continuous favors.

Notes

[1]"I Believe," Cromell Music, Inc., 666 5th Ave., New York, 1952.

[2]*Bulletin of the American Meteorological Society*, 15 March, 1992.

[3]*Los Angeles Times*, 14 March, 1992

[4]Ibid.

[5]Harold Hill, *The Evening Star* (Spencer, Indiana); reprinted in *The Barnacle*, Orange Coast College, California, April 1972.

Tribute to President Harold B. Lee

by Francis M. Gibbons

The qualities of vision, persistence, personal magnetism, and love are the core of President Harold B. Lee's character.

The first one, vision, caused some to call him a "seer," one who saw or understood things others did not. The quality appeared early. When, as a little boy, he was warned by an inner voice not to go across the field to a ruined building, he knew some danger lurked there, and he obeyed. Like a thoroughbred, the gentle rein of that whispered warning was enough to turn him around. Although he did not understand why, he stopped and went the other way, emulating Joseph of old, who also fled from imminent danger. He never questioned or tried to define these spiritual promptings. It was enough he heard and obeyed the inner voice, or saw and followed the inner light that pointed the way.

As President Lee matured, this visionary quality, when coupled with his persistence, produced key changes in Church goals, programs and procedures:

1. The need to provide aid for destitute members of his stake during the depression resulted in a creative local welfare system. It later became the model for a Church-wide welfare program which he directed.
2. His recognition of an imbalance in the relationship between the Priesthood and the auxiliaries, and his resolute efforts to correct it, resulted in the correlation program of the Church.
3. And his understanding of the need to alter the the distribution and communications procedures of a rapidly expanding, global Church, led to sweeping changes in administrative systems at the general headquarters.

In each case, changes occurred only after prolonged planning and follow-through, occasionally in the face of criticism or direct opposition. President Lee persisted to see each one become reality.

Those close to President Lee felt a personal magnetism that drew people to him. His friend, President Marion G. Romney, sensed this the first time they met, being "captivated by his magnetic presence."

There was a spiritual aspect to this phenomenon. It implies a premortal distinction that President Lee had attained and the renowned role he would play on earth. After his call to the Twelve, there was a widespread belief he ultimately would become the prophet. Even before his call, some had that feeling. A sister missionary, for instance, who worked under him in the Colorado Denver Mission, predicted that future for a young Elder Lee. Others who lacked this specific foreknowledge still perceived something about the man that compelled their interest and loyalty, creating a sense of discipleship. One associate described this relationship by saying he always felt like a young athlete in the presence of his coach when around President Lee, wanting to do exactly what he said to do and how to do it, and when to do it. With these disciples, President Lee never had to ask if assignments had been completed. They were anxious to report promptly so he would know they had done what he had asked. Nothing pleased them more than to know he approved of what had been done.

A key aspect of President Lee's personal magnetism that pervaded everything he did was the love he showed toward others. "As my wife and I kneeled in humble prayer," he told the audience at the Mexico Area Conference in August, 1972, "suddenly it seemed as though my mind and heart went out to all three million members throughout the world. I seemed to love every one of them, regardless of their nationality or their color, whether rich or poor or educated or not. I suddenly felt as though they all belonged to me, as though they were all my own brothers and sisters."

This quality of love was evident in every aspect of his short tenure as the President of the Church. Those who associated with him, or who heard him speak, were conscious of it and felt its influence. It was this quality, more than any other fine qualities in his makeup, which set Harold B. Lee apart and gave him special distinction as the Lord's living prophet.

1

Ernest N. Eklof

The Most Dramatic Spiritual Experience of My Life

An example of the gift of tongues for a practical purpose.—H.B.L.

While I was serving as an interpreter at the October 1973 general conference of the Church, I was made aware that some Swedish brethren were attending the conference who had never attended before and perhaps would never come again. I therefore had a great desire that they receive everything the prophet had to deliver. As the General Priesthood meeting began, I had an experience which I have never had before.

Not having a script, I commended myself completely into the hands of the Lord. As President Harold B. Lee began to speak, I was startled by the fact that I knew *beforehand* what he was going to say. The words came in groups before he spoke them. Nevertheless, I dared not translate them and deliver the translation, fearing that some might be my own thoughts. In the past I have usually closed my eyes to better listen, then translated the words in my mind and delivered the interpretation. This time, however, the Spirit told me to not close my eyes, but to keep them on the speaker. Then something almost unbelievable happened.

At President Lee's left temple appeared his thoughts—which were the exact words that had only a moment earlier entered my mind—written in golden letters in an absolutely perfect hand-writing. The letters were about two inches in height and the thickness of writing was about 1/16 of an inch. The words came towards me and passed before my eyes at a distance of somewhat more than twelve inches. They did not appear to be written on anything, but hung as if written in the air. Both the words entering my mind and the writing were in English, exactly as he spoke them moments later. This gave me time to translate his message into Swedish and deliver the interpretation thereof at the very same moment he spoke the words in English from the pulpit.

Not only did I receive the words of his thoughts in my mind and not only did I see the writing, but at the same time I was given the complete understanding of the meaning in English. Never have I felt the inspiration of the Lord more pronounced than I did during this experience. The same experience happened during his closing remarks Sunday afternoon, except that words remained near his temple rather than coming toward me.

After the session ended, I spoke with the Swedish members in attendance. They expressed amazement at what they experienced, telling me that they heard the interpretation and understood enough to realize that the interpreted message was delivered at the same moment Elder Lee spoke the very words in English. They would never forget this "fantastic" experience, they said.

* * *

Elder Lee later read Ernest Eklof's letter describing his remarkable experience at the Quorum meeting of the First Presidency and Council of the Twelve on October 18. Then Elder Lee commented that "Brother Eklof is a reliable, able man, which add[s] weight to his experience." Also, that it was "likely that the experience of the Prophet Joseph Smith in using the Urim and Thummim was similar in some respects to the experience of Brother Eklof."

President N. Eldon Tanner said that a report had come to him that one of the conference visitors who did not speak English said he understood President Lee's talk without the need of a translator.

On October 23, 1973, President Lee wrote to Brother Eklof:

> As I read your spiritual experience in making a direct translation, I had the feeling that your experience must have been similar to that which the Prophet Joseph Smith experienced when he translated the gold plates into English. He must have had about the same kind of thing that was given to you by the Spirit, as words came to him as he concentrated spiritually and saw the meaning and dictated them to the scribe on the other side of the screen.
>
> Thank you for sharing this most sacred experience from you, one of the most dramatic experiences of the gift of tongues that maybe enjoyed by the translators, that I have ever experienced. I do so much appreciate you and thank you for all that you have done and for this confidence that you have entrusted to me. With kindest personal regards—Harold B. Lee

Three days after writing to Brother Eklof, President and Sister Lee were at Ricks College, Rexburg, Idaho, to speak before a studentbody and homecoming audience of over 5,000 persons. In his devotional talk on October 26, 1973, exactly two months before his death, President Lee read Brother Eklof's letter, then provided the following interpretation:

> Latter-day Saints, don't you think for a moment that the Lord does not have means of communicating with us, sending us messages that are beyond our understanding, even to translating an unknown language into our understandable language. He did it with the Prophet Joseph. He did it with King Mosiah. He has done it with others. He will do it today, as we have need. I have no doubt.
>
> My whole soul pleads that I may so live that if the Lord has

any communication that he would wish me to receive for my beloved people that I could be a pure vessel through which that message could come. I do not ask for anything. I do not want anything more than the Lord is willing to send, but I trust that I may live worthy so that I won't be a lame vessel or a broken reed that the Lord cannot use in times when he wants to communicate with his people.

* * *

When Ernest Eklof was contacted over twenty years later, he responded with the following words:

I am humbly grateful for the opportunity to add my personal testimony some 23 years after my experience with the gift of tongues during general conference in October 1973.

For nearly 11 years I served as president of the Swedish Branch of the Church in Salt Lake City. In this capacity, I had many opportunities to host Swedish dignitaries visiting here and to introduce them to our Church leaders. Of course, President Lee was the most desired person to interview during his leadership years. I always received highly complimentary comments after a visit to President Lee's office. Visitors would say, "Mr. Lee seems to be a very powerful man, but at the same time, a very humble and sweet person." That was the President Lee we knew, too.

When President Lee became president of the Church, my stake president called me and told me that I had been called as the president of the Swedish Branch, located in the Salt Lake City Granite Stake, and that I was to be sustained the following Sunday, July 9, 1972. I cannot describe the turmoil my mind experienced at this disclosure. Nevertheless, I sought the Lord in prayer and learned whom He wanted me to choose as my counselors. Trying to settle myself and collect my thoughts on Saturday evening, July 8, 1972, I began reading *The Deseret News* stories about past Church President Joseph Fielding

Smith and the new President Harold B. Lee.

The following morning, July 9, 1972, I woke up a few minutes before 6 a.m. to what may be the most fearful experience of my life. I could, in fact, hear evil spirits speaking to me. The voices told me what a very bad person I was, and they mocked my testimony.

I wondered if I was losing my mind or if I had been possessed by evil forces. The voices continued, "What now, Ernest Eklof, you who had such a strong testimony of Joseph Fielding Smith as your prophet? What now, when he is dead? You don't have a testimony of Harold B. Lee. What do you now have to stand on? And you know you are not the right man to be the president of the Swedish Branch. You realize also that the counselors you've chosen will not support you in that work."

Indeed, I was fearful of losing my mind. My wife was sleeping peacefully so I got out of bed, put on my robe, and went out to the living room. There on the couch was the newspaper with the pictures of President Smith and President Lee. I knelt down and poured out my heart to the Lord and asked Him to deliver me from the powers of Satan. I told the Lord that there was no doubt in my mind that President Harold B. Lee was His true and living prophet on the earth at that time. I told Him that I did not seek for a sign, but that I would gladly receive a firm personal testimony of President Lee as the new, living prophet.

I did not have to wait very long. Suddenly, there came a ray of sunlight, lighting up the picture of President Lee. But the light did not come from outside because the location of the couch was such that no windows or doors were near it. Yet, it was a clear and white light, covering the face of President Lee.

At this moment the evil spirit left me, and my spirit obtained the soft whispering voice of President Joseph Fielding Smith saying, "Rest assured that he, Harold B. Lee, is the mouthpiece of God," repeated three times. At that time a warm, peaceful feeling penetrated my whole body and cen-

tered in my bosom, just the same as I felt when I received my
testimony of the Book of Mormon. Yes, I had received a powerful testimony of President Harold B. Lee as the living
prophet of God on the earth.

To describe my feelings about President Lee, I would borrow from the Book of Mormon reference describing the great
military leader, Moroni:

> Verily, verily I say unto you, if all men had been,
> and were, and ever would be, like unto [President Harold B.
> Lee], behold, the very powers of hell would have been
> shaken forever; yea, the devil would never have power over
> the hearts of the children of men. (Alma 48:17)

I take from my personal journal and life's story these experiences, and I declare with soberness, with God as my witness,
they are indeed true. To this I testify in the sacred name of the
Lord, Jesus Christ. Amen.

*Alderacy dos Santos,
standing for the first time*

Richard R. Tolman

The Faith of a Little Boy

*A testimony of the Elders, of the healing of a five-year-old boy who
had never walked.* Bauru, Brazil, *1959.*—H.B.L.

When I made the decision to go on a mission, an elderly couple in my Bountiful, Utah, ward told me about the marvelous experiences they had while on their mission in Hawaii. They kept telling me that I would be going to Hawaii, and I almost believed them. When I went to Salt Lake for my interview with a General Authority, I had carefully rehearsed a short presentation to give on why I should go to Hawaii. Elder Harold B. Lee interviewed me, and looking deeply into my eyes, as only he could do, asked me, "Will you go where we send you?" I quickly said, "Yes," and that ended my Hawaii aspirations.

I went instead to Brazil. One day, my companion, Elder Darryl M. Jensen, and I were tracting and having little success finding anyone interested in listening to our message. We both felt prompted to continue, in spite of the indifference of the people we were encountering. Then we knocked on the door of the "last house," a small structure located by the side of a large coffee warehouse.

There we met the dos Santos family. They were very poor and had few possessions of a material nature. The father worked at the coffee warehouse loading and unloading 50-kilo sacks of coffee beans from trucks that arrived from the coffee fields. These coffee loaders had a leather shield that they wore on top of their heads and they carried the sacks on their heads, supporting them with their arms. The father was short in stature, perhaps only about 5 feet 2 inches, but the muscles he had built in his arms and neck from carrying these sacks up ladders and loading them in stacks were impressive.

In spite of the humble circumstances in their home—dirt floors in some rooms, no glass in the window openings, and rather crudely made furniture—the father read to his family from the Bible every night. He told us later that when my companion and I came to their door he thought we were the two prophets mentioned in the eleventh chapter of Revelation.

The father welcomed us to his home, asked us to sit down, and called his family together to listen to our message. We could feel the presence of the Spirit as we discussed the gospel with the family. They invited us to return for additional discussions, and we continued to meet with them for about two weeks.

The night before my companion and I were going to leave and travel to Bauru, in the state of São Paulo, we met with them. We told them we were going to Bauru to meet with an apostle of the Lord, Elder Harold B. Lee, and we would be returning with Elder Lee to Londrina (which is in the state of Paraná) where a public meeting would be held.

As we told the family that an apostle would be visiting Londrina, five-year-old Joviniano's face lit up with a huge smile. Although his real name was Alderacy, we all called him Joviniano, which, loosely translated, means "young boy." Joviniano had been born without the use of his legs, and now he looked at his father with new hope.

"When the Apostle comes," he said enthusiastically, "I'll ask him for a blessing and then I'll be able to walk."

The next day, when I met with Elder Lee, I told Elder Lee about Joviniano's desire for a blessing.

"Elder," he replied, "faith like that does not go unrewarded."

We flew from Bauru to Londrina in an old DC-3 of Varig

Airlines with President Sorensen, some elders from the mission home, and President and Sister Lee. Upon arriving in Londrina, we checked Elder and Sister Lee into a hotel so they could freshen up, and then went down to the rented house that was used both for a chapel and a residence for my companion and me. The dos Santos family was one of the first to arrive. I don't remember any of the details of Elder Lee's sermon that night, but I do remember how strongly the Spirit was felt by everyone who was there, members and nonmembers alike.

After the meeting, we introduced the family to Elder Lee and we went into the branch president's office where I anointed Joviniano and Elder Lee sealed the anointing with a powerful blessing. The Spirit's influence was so strong in the room I thought my back bone was going to crawl off my body. Some of the details of the blessing have slipped from my memory, but I do remember some of the more powerful words that Elder Lee pronounced on Joviniano that night. He rebuked the illness that was in his body and commanded strength into the muscles and bones of his legs. I specifically remember the word "rebuke" because, at that time, that was the only word he used whose equivalent in Portuguese I did not know. Nevertheless, the Spirit was very helpful in obtaining an exact translation for the family to understand.

When Elder Lee had finished, tears were seen in the eyes of every person in the room. He gave Joviniano a big hug and placed him in his father's arms.

The next day we visited the family, and the father proudly showed us that Joviniano could now stand shakily on his own two legs for the first time in his life. I telephoned the mission home with the good news and they promised to relay the message to President Sorensen and Elder Lee.

In the city of Porto Alegre, as Elder Lee was about ready to leave Brazil and go to Uruguay, he bore a powerful testimony describing Joviniano's miraculous healing. The effect of his powerful parting testimony quickly spread throughout the Brazilian

South Mission and greatly stimulated the work.

After dividing the mission, Elder Lee brought President and Sister Sorensen back to Brazil to preside over the Brazilian South Mission. At the time we were a very small mission; we had, I believe, about 1,000 members in the entire mission. He promised us that the number would soon double, which it did.

In my letter to the mission president in October 1959, I reported that Joviniano, whose legs were once useless limbs hanging from his body, was gaining more strength daily and learning how to use his legs. By December, Joviniano was walking and still making excellent progress. His parents had been baptized and were faithfully keeping the commandments.

Long after I returned home from my mission, I continued to ask returning missionaries if they had labored in Londrina and if they knew the dos Santos family. The missionaries who had had contact with the dos Santos family were invariably positive about the contributions to the branch by this unforgettable family.

Notes
[1]Brother Tolman, the missionary in this story of 34 years ago, is now professor of zoology at Brigham Young University.

3

Daniel T. Bogdan

From Behind a Closed Door

The Holy Ghost radiated from a room occupied by Elder Lee during a 1963 Seattle Stake Conference, and testified to a nonmember in the hallway.

In my youth, my kind, wise mother taught me of the existence of God and the teachings of the Bible. I learned to pray to the God of Abraham, Isaac and Jacob, but in my ignorance I failed to see His guidance and wisdom.

As I grew older, my life became filled with anger, frustrations, and ambitions that I had no idea how to achieve. My life was empty and meaningless. Pains of an ulcer plagued me for ten years and constantly made me wonder if the only purpose of life was to be miserable.

In time I married, and my wife and I attended various churches and congregations. I always felt ill at ease. I saw sermons as "intellectual duels," for I could find no logic or purpose in the existence of mankind or even my existence. In some cases, I found churches that were no more than social events and association, which seemed to be the justification for their existence; they rarely spoke of Christ's life and teachings, though they used His name.

At my place of employment I observed a particular young man. I admired his emotional control and the way he conducted himself. Someone said he was a "Mormon." Curious, I asked him for some literature on the "Mormon Church," and he gave me a Book of Mormon. However, I found the reading so difficult and the world it presented to me so foreign and full of strange names, I placed the book on the bookshelf and did not continue my reading. My friend later transferred to another part of the country.

Although my work and studies filled the next year, I nevertheless continued to feel a desire and intent to return to and read that unusual book. One day a new employee was hired to work in our office. I learned that he was a returned missionary from Holland, but I did not speak with him about the Book of Mormon that had been given me earlier. However, in time he was assigned to me, and he spoke to me of the Church. Although I was reluctant and skeptical of some of his teachings, I accepted his offer when he invited my wife and me to attend the Seattle Stake Conference in March 1963.

We arrived early for the afternoon conference session, and my friend took me on a tour of the building. I could sense his pride as he ushered me through the building—to the cultural hall and the Relief Society rooms, past the baptismal font, then through the Sunday School wing. I arrogantly thought the building was nice although it seemed full of noisy people who appeared to be all moving at the same time, and I was beginning to be bored.

As my friend led me down a crowded and noisy hallway that outwardly seemed no different than the others we had traversed, a different kind of feeling came over me. We walked to the end of the hallway and passed a closed door and I felt a warmth radiate out from within that room, like the warmth of a comfortable fire. As we walked away, this comfort dissipated, and I wondered what could it be.

To return to where our wives were waiting, we had to walk past that room again. Once more I felt a comfort that I had never before known, only to feel it wane as we moved down the hall. I wanted to bask again in this great spirit and enjoy the happiness and comfort I felt near that door and so I excused myself to

return for a drink of water as the route would require me to walk
a third time past the room from which this wonderful spirit radiated. How I wanted to rush in and find the source of that exquis-
ite feeling. It was there in the midst of a crowded hall, unaware
of those who passed me, that I stumbled in the field and found
the "pearl" that changed my life.

I was told later that Elder Harold B. Lee, the visiting authority at that conference, was in that room, and since that day I have
learned that great and noble men live today: men who live their
lives with one purpose and one goal—to share their knowledge
and to lead others into the presence of a loving God and His Son,
Jesus Christ. Never, never had I dreamed that such a great and
noble man would cross the paths of my life! How grateful I am
for that day!

Since that day my life changed, and I found meaning and purpose for my existence. My frustrations remain great, but they no
longer rule my life. My ulcers plague me no more, my outlook is
positive, and my ambitions have become focused—for I have
found and understand a great plan and a most meaningful goal!
I can truthfully say my blessings are many. They all originate
from a living God!

For many years I felt the desire to thank Elder Lee in person
for what he gave me in 1963 and express my deep respect and
gratitude. At last I wrote him and received his prompt reply.

                                        August 26, 1968

Dear Brother Bogdan:

    Needless to say, I was humbled by your letter and your tes-
timony in which I had some part. I hasten to explain to you
that any of us, you included, who live true to [our] covenants
[with God], may likewise extend a radiance of influence to all
with whom they come in contact.

    May the Lord's blessings continue to be with you as you
enlarge your understanding in the scope of your authority as a
holder of the Holy Priesthood and one who has a right to the

gift of the Holy Ghost as a baptized member.

With kindest personal regards and ever praying the blessings of the Lord upon you, I am

Faithfully yours,
Harold B. Lee

I shall always be grateful and look upon Harold B. Lee as a friend. His life was a source of marvelous strength to me. I give thanks to my God, for all that He has restored through his love—His prophets, His great plan which gives understanding, meaning, and purpose to life, His true Church, which provides growth, service, and the restored gospel.

Though 31 years has passed and life's lessons continue, the miraculous event involving Elder Lee leading to my conversion was the beginning from which I have drawn great strength and determination.

4

*Jesus sent out his disciples,
[saying,] "Heal the sick, cleanse
the lepers, raise the dead..."*

Matt 10:8

Mrs. Leon F. Liddell

"Raised from the Dead"—H.B.L.

*This story, titled "The Open Grave—A Story of Faith" was pub-
lished in the* Church News *on 16 May 1948. Accompanying the
article written by Mrs. Leon F. Liddell was a photograph of the
Eti Te'o family posed with Elder Lee.*

When Elder Matthew Cowley of the Council of the Twelve
visited our stake, he told us many beautiful stories of the great
faith of the Samoan people and of the earnest desire of many of
these Saints to visit the temple in Hawaii. In response, many present sincerely hoped to be of assistance to these wonderful people in their effort to visit the Hawaiian Temple, so far away from
their little island.

The opportunity to assist them came quite unexpectedly in
June 1947 when the M-Men/Gleaner convention for Northern
California and Nevada met in San Francisco. Participating were
560 young people from seven stakes and one mission. There was
quite a sum of money left over the estimated cost of the convention, and with the memory of Elder Cowley's talk still burning in
their hearts, the stake representatives of these young people
decided to donate the entire amount ($790) to Elder Cowley to
assist these faithful island people to visit the temple.

The opportunity to meet some of these amazing Samoan
Latter-day Saints came unexpectedly as well. We were especially
thrilled to know Eti Te'o, a chief from the village of Mapusaga,

Samoa, who came to make his home in San Francisco. Eti told us the following story from his youth.

At eighteen he was living in the village of Pago Pago helping to translate the Doctrine and Covenants into Samoan. A friend of his named George came to the village to work as a carpenter. After about three months he became very sick and was taken to the Navy Hospital where he stayed six months. He grew steadily worse and one morning asked his uncle to send for the Mormon elders to administer to him or he would die. His uncle refused, saying it could do no good since not even the doctors had not been able to help him.

George then called the nurse. "If I die," he asked, "please send a note to the elders and have my body taken to the mission home." At 7:30 that night George died. Eti recalled:

> The next morning I was passing the hospital on my way to work when the nurse called to me. She was crying when she told me what had happened. I immediately took the news to Brother Lopati at the mission home, and he asked me to go behind the house and start digging the grave. I had dug [to a depth of] about two-and-a-half feet when he came to me and said, "Put the shovel back. We are going to the hospital to see George."
>
> It was now 10 o'clock in the morning. I could not understand what he wanted to go to the hospital for, but I put the shovel back and went with him.
>
> George was laying in an outer room where the dead were kept and as we passed it I could see *lagomea* (flies that cover dead bodies) all over the windows, and I was angry with Brother Lopati.
>
> "Don't you think we will disgrace the Church by doing this?" I questioned him, but he went right on into the hospital. We were not allowed to enter the room where George lay—both the nurse and the doctor told us that if we entered it we would be sent to jail.

Brother Lopati sent for his wife and two other elders and after kneeling in prayer they signed a paper, one by one, signifying that they would willingly go to jail after entering George's room.

Eti could not bring himself to sign the paper as he had no desire to go to jail. Brother Lopati came up to him and told him that he had been promised in his patriarchal blessing that if he lived right he would have power to raise the dead. He also said that they must wait for him—that it was urgent for him to witness this event. At 12 o'clock noon Eti finally signed the paper, and they all went in beside George's bed.

Brother Lopati unwrapped the gauze from his face and we all knelt by his bedside.

I remember only three words he spoke as he lay his hands on the boy's head. They were, "George, come back."' He spoke a few words further, then said, "Amen."

George sneezed and began to breathe. His first words were, "I would like a cup of rice." Then he sat up and said, "I heard your voice from a long distance."

I ran from the room—shaking all over. Running down the halls, I kept saying, almost hysterically, "George wants a cup of rice!" over and over. I rushed into Dr. Lane's office without knocking and could only say, "George wants a cup of rice!" He hurried back with me and when he saw George sitting up talking, he was speechless. He could not speak for a long time, then he slowly walked over to the bedside to examine George. After a few minutes he stated that the boy was normal and his heart action was perfect.

Turning to Brother Lopati, Dr. Lane said, "No one but God could do that." He asked us to come to his house later and we stayed there all the rest of the day answering his questions. He joined the Church in due time, as did several other hospital workers.

Now, twenty-three years later, George is in good health and lives in the village of Aua, Samoa—but his story will not be forgotten. The open grave is still there back of the mission home near where I live. I keep it just as I left it that day. I want my children and grandchildren to see it and know this story.

5

Lu Gene H. Neuenswander

Heart Petals

At the Los Angeles Temple dedication the Savior replaced Elder Lee while he was leading the Hosannah shout.

In 1956 my husband and I had the privilege of attending the Los Angeles Temple dedication. At this time Doug was attending dental school at the University of Southern California. I worked part-time at the seminary office located by the university campus. Ray Jones, Paul Dunn, and Lyman Berrett were the seminary directors.

Doug and I sat in the terrestrial room and watched the dedication on television. As Elder Lee explained the Hosanna Shout and began to lead it, I saw the Savior appear where Elder Lee was standing. So great was the spirit that I thought it entirely normal that He should be there and I had no doubt that everyone present could see Him as clearly as I could. I wanted to share my joy with my husband, but I felt that I couldn't interrupt the Hosanna Shout. The Savior was clothed in a white robe and was the most glorious being I have ever conceived of. My whole being was thrilled.

When we sat down, I turned to my husband and exclaimed, "Isn't it wonderful the Savior was with us today?"

My husband looked at me curiously. "I didn't see Him," he said.

* * *

I have been given the blessing of dreams, discernment, and prophecy. These gifts aren't always easy ones to be blessed with. We have had many miracles and faith-promoting experiences in our family. My children have powerful testimonies of the Savior, which I feel is a result of my own manifestation.

Although I have shared this story with very few people until now, the feeling I received from this wonderful manifestation has never left me. I felt both unworthy and yet grateful to the Lord. I felt it must feel like heaven to be in the presence of my Savior. The feeling that came to me was a desire to live worthily so when I complete this life on earth I can go into His presence and receive that feeling again. I would give everything to live a good life to receive that blessing. Elder Melvin J. Ballard's words describe how I felt in seeing the Savior:

> I cannot begin this night to tell you what that means—to enjoy the blessings and privileges of dwelling in Christ's presence forever and ever. I know how the soul is thrilled; I know the feeling that comes by being in his presence for but a moment. I would give all that I am, all that I hope to be, to have the joy of his presence, to dwell in his love and affection and to be in favor with the Master of all things forever and ever.[1]

I felt I needed to share this experience with Elder Lee himself, and on October 30, 1962, while traveling through Salt Lake City, I had opportunity to speak with him. When I told him of my manifestation, tears came to his eyes. He asked if he could have it recorded and asked his secretary to come in and transcribe my experience. The title, "Heart Petals," was his recommendation.

Since our meeting, Elder Lee has come to be closely associated with the Savior in my mind. I felt, too, that perhaps it gave him faith and courage. He is such a spiritual and Christlike man. I think he understands how I feel about beginning to get a glimpse of the path Jesus walked.

This manifestation has made me always feel very humble and has helped me to have the faith to endure. I know that He sustains me. I will try to serve Him to the best of my ability. I know that my Redeemer lives. Through the atonement of Christ, I know that all mankind may be saved. I accept the divinity of the mission of Jesus as the Savior of the world. May His spirit enable me to endure to the end, faithful to Him.

Notes

1 *Sermons and Missionary Services of Melvin Joseph Ballard,* by Bryant S. Hinckley (SLC: Deseret Book, 1949), p. 245.

6

Veda J. Porter Mortimer

Priesthood Power

The power of the Lord, not man, commits to a patriarch his keys and authority to bless and foretell.—H.B.L.

Elder Harold B. Lee visited my Manhattan Ward, in the New York Stake, in September 1959, and afterwards, several ward members joined him in the bishop's office in the basement to be set apart and ordained to new callings.

As it is not a large room, the twenty people in it filled it almost completely. A chair was set in the center of the bishop's office. Brother DeWitt Paul took a seat on the chair in the center of the room, his back toward the door. Elder Lee took his place behind Brother Paul to give him the ordination and blessing as the newly called stake patriarch. Just as Elder Lee lifted his hands to place them on Brother Paul's head, I both saw and felt a shaft of bright light come onto the back and top of Elder Lee's head. It was like bright sunshine suddenly coming through a square window, eight to ten inches square, and shining down on a 45-degree angle on the back and top of his head. It was as if a shade had suddenly been drawn to let in the bright sun.

As a bowed my head, I saw the light and thought, "What a coincidence that that shaft of bright sunlight should shine on Elder Lee just at the particular instant that he was putting his hands on Brother Paul's head."

Just as quickly as I thought this, I realized there was no window in the office, and therefore it could not be sunlight. The only opening in the room was the door, which was closed. A small fan was the only source of ventilation. In the same instant I understood that it was a stream of light from heaven, a light that needed no physical window to enter the room.

When I opened my eyes and looked up to see the shaft of light, my eyes could no longer see the light. Nevertheless, I knew the light was still there, for Brother Paul was receiving information and advice that could come only from the Lord. I knew the light was still there and still in use, even though I could no longer see it.

I know that there are literal windows in heaven through which blessings and inspiration can come, as Malachi says. I understand now how patriarchs can give blessings and how sacred ordinances can be performed with the help of the Lord. I am most grateful to the Lord for the privilege of this experience.

* * *

On December 5, 1969, at an LDSSA Youth Conference, Elder Lee read Veda Mortimer's letter describing her experience. Then he added his own interpretation as a lesson to youth, saying:

> "In other words, I was laying my hands upon the head of Brother DeWitt Paul and the Lord was laying his hands upon Brother Paul's head by a humble servant who bore the Holy Priesthood. So it is with you who exercise your priestly responsibility in whatever you do—when you baptize, when you administer the sacrament, when you bless the sick, or when you confirm membership. Whatever priesthood rites—it is as though the Lord was putting his hands upon you or upon that one whom you bless by your own act. That's priesthood power."

7

E. La Mar Buckner

Youth Responds to Spiritual Truths

On the rare occasion when Elder Lee preached from his "Miracle File," another miracle occurred. An entire audience remained silent in their seats after the benediction, still overcome by the Spirit.

While I was serving as a member of the Latter-day Saint Student Association International Committee, under Elders Paul H. Dunn and Marion D. Hanks, we held our second International Convention at the Hotel Utah. During the meetings we heard from various leaders from the LDSSA and the general auxiliaries of the Church.

At a reception held in the Church offices on Thursday, we met and shook hands with President N. Eldon Tanner, President Harold B. Lee, Bishop Robert L. Simpson, Young Men's Superintendent W. Jay Eldredge, Young Women's President Florence Jacobson, Sunday School Superintendent David L. McKay, Elder Hanks, and other LDSSA leaders.

In my journal I noted that "Elder Lee stood in line leaning against the wall and a sofa as he shook hands." Elder Lee had undergone two major surgical operations in the previous year and had not yet fully recovered from the latest one. Brother Hanks had afterwards commented to me that he had been concerned about Brother Lee being able to hold up during the reception.

On Friday night, a banquet was held and a large crowd of between 250 and 300 people was present at the LDS Institute of Religion at the University of Utah. They were the youth leaders of nearly 300 college campuses from America, England, and the Hawaiian Islands. Following the banquet we adjourned into the chapel. There we sang, "We Thank Thee, O God, for a Prophet." During the opening song Elder Harold B. Lee stood up and left the stand. Seeing him leave, I wondered if he would be unable to speak to us that night.

Elder Hanks introduced the guests, then introduced Elder Lee, telling us of his illness.

"I had almost hoped that Elder Lee had not accepted our invitation to be present at last night's reception, that he might conserve his strength for tonight," he said. He then introduced Elder Lee with the scripture found in Alma 48:11-12: "He was a strong and a mighty man; he was a man of perfect understanding ... a man who did labor exceedingly for the welfare and safety of his people."

That evening, after President Lee's sermon, I was so impressed by his entire spirit that when I returned to my hotel room I immediately wrote my feelings in my journal. I dated the entry December 6, 1959.

> I want to try and record while fresh in my mind the events of the last few days and the events of last night in particular....
>
> [After he was introduced] Elder Lee walked slowly to the pulpit and softly began to speak. One was almost required to strain and to lean forward to hear him. With each sentence, however, there was evidence of resurgent strength as this "special witness to Jesus Christ" bore testimony of [his] remarkable experiences....
>
> [He said] that since his call to the General Authorities, 28 years ago, he had witnessed 30 of his companions being called home. He especially emphasized the two occasions when the Prophets of the Lord were called home. He then reported how

impressed he was when he saw President George Albert Smith speak at the funeral of his predecessor, President Heber J. Grant, and how the mantle of the Lord fell upon him and transformed the Apostle to become the Prophet.

He told about his lonely experience in conducting a funeral service honoring his fellow apostle Charles A. Callis in Florida, and how just as the brethren were in their temple robes praying for him in the Salt Lake Temple, at that very moment in Florida he felt a rush and strength of the Holy Spirit....

He related an experience of where a man's injured arm was healed while shaking hands with Elder Lee. That man later joined the Church. He added, this was not by Elder Lee's doing but by the power of the Lord....

With each passing minute he [became] stronger and stronger, drawing us all closer to the Lord. At the close, he bore his testimony that God lives and told how as a special witness of Jesus this truth had been revealed to him. Everyone knew, too, that he knew.... It seemed that waves of the Spirit of the Lord were passing over the audience.

After Elder Lee's sermon, the benediction was given by a young man, a converted atheist. In his unique prayer he pledged and committed to God the determination of all the youth there to sustain and support those principles that had been taught at the conference. Previously, this same young man had been heard to express criticism, complaining that solid answers were lacking. Now, however, he concluded his prayer by pledging his unqualified support of what had been taught and asking the youth of the Church to do likewise.

When he returned to his seat the meeting was formally over but not a soul stirred. The sound of silence was deafening. The silence lasted perhaps ten minutes, although to me it felt much longer. Even when Elder Hanks went to the pulpit he said nothing, thus allowing the overpowering spirit to continue through the chapel. I could see tears in the eyes of Elder

Lee, Elder Richard L. Evans, and their wives, and in the eyes of students in the congregation....

When several of these individuals who had been on the stand [stood up to leave], the remainder of the audience rose to their feet but remained standing silently while Elders Lee and Evans and their wives left.

As they left, Brother Marvin Higbee, who had so beautifully sung "I Walked Today Where Jesus Walked," began to sing "The Spirit of God Like a Fire Is Burning." The congregation joined him, but it soon faded out for even this sacred song was viewed as an encroachment upon the pervasive spirit.

It was to me a manifestation unequalled to anything I had before seen. Elder Lee had borne testimony as I had seldom heard. He said that God raises men who are needed from time to time to meet His needs.... With all of the campus unrest at present, it is easy to see God's hand in preparing the Latter-day Saints Student Association to meet the challenges that are now and will yet arise facing our beloved youth....

I felt the students were responding to the testimony of Elder Lee, giving their support with silence. The spirit there was felt by all and it was one of the greatest witnesses that I had ever seen of the work of the Holy Ghost, to testify of the truthfulness of an apostolic sermon.

As we left the chapel we were surprised to see Elder Lee and his wife standing in the foyer shaking hands with each and every one of those in the chapel as they filed by, still not speaking but openly weeping. The strength of Elder Harold B. Lee was still being transmitted to us, as we shook hands with an apostle of God.

Although a dance had been planned to follow this meeting, the overwhelming response was that no dance was desired. "We just want to go to our rooms and think about this marvelous experience," each person would say. Although the orchestra for the dance had already arrived, they were dismissed.

The next day I had the opportunity to see Elder Lee for a few moments and commented how impressed I had been with his sermon. I told him that I had gone to my hotel room and written many pages of notes of my impressions of what he had said so I would remember what I had felt.

A few days later I received a telephone call from Elder Lee's office. The purpose of his call was to ask a favor of me. Would I send to him the notes that I had made following his talk at the conference, he asked, explaining that he had been invited to travel to Harvard University to give much the same message that he had given at this conference, to the LDS student leaders on campus in Cambridge. His health would not permit him to do so, but he had agreed to talk to the students by a telephone hook-up. Elder Lee said that since his message had been under the direction of the Holy Spirit, he was not at all certain as to what he had said at the conference. He asked if I would mail my unedited notes that very day; otherwise, his secretary would not have sufficient time to type them.

"I doubt you'll be able to read my writing," I told him, "but you're welcome to my notes." Elder Lee assured me that they would be adequate, then expressed appreciation to me for having recorded my feelings concerning his message in a way that might be helpful for his next assignment.

Years later I learned that my humble scribbled notes found an honored resting place in President Lee's "Miracle File" where they were kept for 34 years! How little do we know the mysteries and workings of God upon us.

* * *

I have many other memories of my association with President Lee. On one occasion I was in President Lee's office when he was a counselor in the First Presidency, and he showed me his small day-book that was about four by seven inches in size and typical of those maintained by most businessmen at that time. He had filled many of them over the years. In them he made his daily entries as to his feelings and activities. I was greatly impressed with this remarkable man who was so intensely busy, yet would always make the time to enter his daily activities and feelings in his journal.

One lasting lesson frames the Church's policy with regard to politics. In early 1960 my name was mentioned frequently in the newspapers and in other circles as a possible candidate for U.S. Congress. I had advised my friends and associates that I was not in a position to accept their support since my calling as bishop had carried with it the obligation of building a new chapel and stake center. I felt that this was a priority that could not be put aside for politics.

One day Utah Governor George Dewey Clyde made an appointment for me to come to his office, and when I arrived he immediately took me to the headquarters building of the Church. Soon, to my surprise, we were in the office of Elder Harold B. Lee.

Governor Clyde told Elder Lee that his associates thought it would be well for me if I talked to Elder Lee as they were interested in having me run for Congress.

Elder Lee was most judicious and wise in the counsel and guidance that he gave to me. He immediately explained that he was not representing the Church in talking with me. He went on further to explain that he would never talk anyone into running for political office, even his own son, against his personal will.

He then told a story of one of his own experiences in politics, since he had been a city commissioner in Salt Lake City before he became a general authority of the Church. On one occasion he had been invited by some political leaders to meet with the members of the First Presidency. President J. Rueben Clark, Jr., speaking for the First Presidency, told Elder Lee that many individuals had mentioned Elder Lee's name in terms of the office of United States Senator. He went on to add that it was the First Presidency's understanding that if they would give their approval,

Elder Lee would be willing to become a candidate.

"I corrected President Clark," said Elder Lee. "I told him that his statement was not accurate. I said, 'If you will forgive me for saying so, President Clark, I have told my friends that I would only run for U. S. Senator if I were *told to do so* by the First Presidency.'"

"Oh," said President Clark, "That is quite a different story." He went on to say that the First Presidency would never tell a man to run for office.

"That is not our responsibility or prerogative," he continued. "We do look with favor upon having good men run for office from all religions and faiths, and we are pleased when good men of both parties, who are members of the Church, make themselves available for political office."

As I sat with with the governor, Elder Lee concluded, "As a result of this conversation, I never became a candidate for the U.S. Senate, since it was not the responsibility of the First Presidency to tell men to run for political office. I have told you this story to explain that it is still our practice not to tell you to run for office. I would, however, tell you that should you desire to run for political office as a Congressman we would look with favor upon you, or any other member of the Church who is in good standing, to become such a candidate."

At this, I explained to the governor that my heavy Church responsibilities as a bishop prevented my entering into a political campaign of the magnitude that being a candidate for Congress would require. Elder Lee reassured me that he accepted my decision and was certain that others would do so also.

I am grateful for the influence and example of this great prophet of the Lord. President Harold B. Lee was truly a chosen vessel.

8

Francis M. Gibbons

Our Miracle Girl

Mother saved in child-bearing. Baby safe. Father devoted a life of service as though trying to pay interest on a "great debt" to a merciful Father.—H.B.L.

My wife, Helen, and I first met Elder Harold B. Lee in Palo Alto, California, in 1948 while I was attending Stanford University. We belonged to a study group that included President Lee's daughter, Maurine, and her husband, Ernie Wilkins, who also was a Stanford student. Usually, when Elder Lee had a conference assignment in that area, the Wilkinses would arrange a meeting of the study group in their home, where we were privileged to receive counsel and instruction from Elder Lee in an intimate, relaxed setting.

At the time, we were childless, although we had been married for several years. In early 1950, during one of his visits to Palo Alto, Helen felt inspired to seek a blessing from Elder Lee. In it he blessed her that the vital functions of her body would be quickened by the Holy Spirit to begin the processes which would result in motherhood. He specifically blessed her, "even as Hannah of old," and counselled her to covenant with the Lord in her secret prayers as Hannah had done. He blessed her also with peace of mind and faith and that if there should be a space of time before she conceived that we should spend that time in service to the Church, to open our hearts to other children and to prove ourselves worthy of parenthood. He conferred also a special blessing on the doctors who would serve her, that they would be specially inspired in exercising their medical skills in her behalf.

We endeavored, as best we could, to comply with all the conditions Elder Lee had mentioned. We were very active in the ward, filling assignments in Relief Society and Sunday School. We did baby-sitting for our friends, took Helen's young brother into our home, and even applied to adopt a baby through the California placement service. As far as we can determine, Helen conceived about the time of our visit to the California State agency in San Francisco.

Everything went well with the pregnancy until about three weeks before the expected delivery, when Helen developed a severe pain in her side. The doctor thought her complaints were merely the reaction of a woman pregnant for the first time, who did not realize what to expect in carrying a child. Nevertheless, after the complaints continued, he hospitalized Helen to conduct tests, which revealed nothing.

The evening before the baby's birth, the doctor visited Helen in the hospital again, and, finding no clues to the root of her trouble, went home. He later told us that he became uneasy as he thought about Helen, and that he felt compelled to return to the hospital. When he arrived and examined her again, he discovered that the baby was in distress, which caused him to decide immediately on a Caesarean section. The doctor contacted me at home to obtain my consent. I barely had time to arrange for a neighbor, Mac VanValkenburg, to accompany me to the hospital where we administered to Helen.

After the doctor had taken the baby, he discovered the root of Helen's pain. Somehow, circulation had been cut off to one ovary, resulting in a strangulated ovary. By that time, the lack of circulation had caused the ovary, and all the surrounding tissue, to become gangrenous, requiring its removal. Had he induced labor as he had thought to do earlier in the evening, or had there been a delay of as much as a half hour in taking the baby, it is almost certain that Suzi would have been born dead or with serious brain damage because of the lack of oxygen, and Helen would have lost her life.

After the delivery, a nurse told Helen that someone should go to church the next day, Sunday, and thank God that she and the baby were alive and well, which I did, for it was Fast Sunday.

A few months after the birth, I wrote Elder Lee a letter, detailing the circumstances of Suzi's miraculous birth and of the unusual way in which his blessing to Helen had been fulfilled.

Many years later, and shortly after I began my service with the First Presidency as their executive secretary, President Lee said one morning before a First Presidency meeting that he had been looking through his "Miracle File" and had found the letter I had written to him almost 20 years before, telling about Helen's blessing and Suzi's birth.

The day before President Lee's death, he called me at home to wish me and the family a merry Christmas. Almost the last words I ever heard him speak in mortality were to ask, "How is our miracle girl?" I understand that experiences of this kind were repeated time and again during President Lee's ministry. He was and is a true prophet of God, richly endowed with spiritual perceptions and sensitivities possessed by few of God's servants.

When "our miracle girl" was sealed to Timothy A. Burton in February, 1972, in the Salt Lake Temple, President Lee graciously performed the ceremony.

Suzanne is now a 44-year-old mother of five children. The passing years have increased her awe at the power of President Harold B. Lee's blessing. She is assured his prophetic words enlightened the mind and guided the hands of the doctor who delivered her.

The incident has imbued Suzanne with a sense of indebtedness and with a resolve to make the most of the life her mother's travail, President Lee's inspiration, and the doctor's skill preserved for her. Through the years this has been reflected in an unusual zest and enthusiasm for any task or project.

While managing her household and giving loving care to her husband and children, she completed her university studies, graduating with honors. Her Church work, which has been constant, has included administrative and teaching duties in Young Women, Primary, Relief Society and Sunday School, as well as a much-loved assignment as choir director.

Additionally, to help insure the proper care and education of her children, she carved out a career in communications while juggling her many other duties. For several years she was the morning anchor and reported on Idaho's largest radio station. At present, she is the public information officer and assistant to the mayor of Boise, Idaho.

Her greatest joys and satisfactions, however, come from the loving relationship with her husband, Timothy A. Burton, an environmental scientist, whose support and cooperation have made their work-filled lives manageable.

Their common goal is to teach their children the power and reality of God and His willingness, through spiritual means, to touch and influence their lives in the same way their mother was immeasurably blessed through the inspired words of a living prophet.

9

*"Stretching forth thine
hand to heal..."*

Matt 10:8

*A.M.L.

A Blessing Through a Car Window

*Elder Lee blessed the mother of an ailing four-year-old through the
window of an automobile, and her son, Lee, at home is healed.*

It was April 15, 1973. As I stood waiting for conference to
start at the New Jersey Stake Center, a brother passed by. "Won't
you take a seat?" he asked.

"No," I told him. "The seats are too far away and I want to be
as close to the Prophet as possible. I stood in line at General
Conference for two hours when I was expecting my third child
after driving all night from California." I knew if I could do that,
I could stand for the conference. That was how much I wanted
to be near him. At one point, a chair near me became vacant and
I was able to sit through the rest of the conference.

When the Prophet stood up to speak I could feel the spirit
become very strong within me. When it was announced that
President Lee would shake hands with people, I knew I had to get
to him. As we sang the last song, I began to cry and could hardly
sing.

After the closing prayer, people poured forward to see him.
When he said he would have to leave, I knew that would be as
close as I would get to him. Still, I felt such a strong urge to get
to him somehow. I watched to see which way he would leave the
building, but lost him in the crowd.

I went outside and looked around for him. I saw where the

people were clustered and moved toward the parking lot. His car was completely surrounded. As I waited, I spoke briefly with some missionaries from our ward, then someone asked me to move so the car with President Lee could back out. I stood about three feet away from the car as it passed by. Disheartened, I thought that would be the closest I would get to him.

My car was parked down the road from the stake center, and as I began to walk to it, I watched as the car with President Lee drew up near my car. I quickly crossed the street, expecting his car to pull away at any moment. I finally passed his car and went to mine.

I stood there and thought to myself, "Should I go stand by his car?" A myriad of scriptures crossed my mind. No, I decided, it would be unfair to bother him. Then a force turned my body around and gave me the strength and courage to approach his car.

As I walked up to his window, President Lee rolled it down partway.

"Would you shake my hand for my son?" I asked him. "He couldn't come today because his foot is in a cast." My four-year-old son had a great admiration for the prophet because his name is Lee and that has a special significance to him. Lee had hurt his foot playing and the doctor put a cast on and warned my son to stay off the foot for the next two weeks. Lee wanted to get up and play and so had ruined the cast after only two days. The doctor and I were both afraid that his foot wouldn't heal properly. That morning my son complained of pain in his casted foot so he had stayed home.

President Lee took my hand and shook it, then continued to hold it. "I bless your son," he said, "that his foot will heal properly and correctly with no deformities." His voice was very soft and kind, gentle and compassionate.

I was so emotionally overcome I don't remember if I even had the presence of mind to thank him. I do remember that my body lost all feeling. Back in my car, I put my head down and cried, thanking the Lord that such an unworthy servant as I had this special experience and blessing for my son. I cried halfway home before I was able to compose myself.

At home my four-year-old son told me his foot didn't hurt anymore. I told him what happened and he smiled. "President Lee gave me a blessing from you," he said. "Now we can take my cast off."

The next day I called the doctor and made an appointment. The doctor looked at Lee's foot. "The cast needs to come off," he said. When the cast was off, he pressed on the area where the fracture was. "Does that hurt?"

"No," said Lee. The doctor looked disbelieving. "Well, it looks like it's healed. The foot will probably swell and you'll feel a lump, but don't worry. Just call me if your son has any trouble." But nothing of the kind happened, nor did Lee have any trouble with his foot after that.

I thank the Lord for this miracle and for the faith of a small, red-headed, freckled-faced four-year-old boy—my son, Lee.

*Initials only used at author's request.

10

Doris Elaine Simpson Crew

Vision of a Future Prophet

She had a vision of Elder Lee replacing President David O. McKay at the Los Angeles Temple dedication.

Ever since the elders taught the gospel of Jesus Christ in our home, the temple has seemed the greatest gift (outside of Jesus Christ) that the Lord can give His children; the eternal family unit, to look forward to and to prepare to dwell with our Creator, is magnificent to anticipate.

My husband and I attended the dedication of the Los Angeles Temple in 1956. It was our first time in the temple together. While President David O. McKay was giving the dedicatory prayer, the Spirit directed me to look up twice, but each time I couldn't as the prayer was being said. Finally, on the third impression, I had enough courage to open my eyes. I saw President McKay giving the prayer, then I saw him being replaced by Elder Harold B. Lee. The voice continued, the prayer was going on, but Elder Lee took the Prophet's place for several seconds. It was long enough so that I knew that in due time he would be the future prophet on the earth.

As I thanked the Lord for such a divine experience, I was overwhelmed that one so simple as I could have been given such a testimony the first time in His holy temple. Perhaps the vision was given so that I would endure to the end and not fall by the wayside when the road becomes rougher and the challenges greater.

This experience is still vivid in my memory after 28 years. It has been a powerful testimony to me of how the Lord loves each child of His, and how He gives strong bonds of enlightenment to keep them true and faithful. Many times Satan has tried to pull me down to despair but the Savior's love and deep commitment to me has kept me going. I have since learned that others had visions in the Los Angeles Temple dedicatory sessions. I suppose they were given for the same reason as mine, as a comfort and assurance to help keep us faithful to the end.

At one time I shared my rare experience with my mother, although she was not a member, and she did live to see Harold B. Lee become president of the Church. At that time she said, "Honey, if I ever join a church, I will become a Mormon."

This last October I was baptized for my mother by proxy in the Oakland Temple. While waiting to do her ordinance I heard beautiful music. It was a symphony orchestra playing. I thought the music was on a tape being piped into the room, but I later found out that no music was on tape or being played into the area. Mother loved music and adored the Tabernacle Choir. The Lord gave us music at her baptism, for which I am most grateful.

Douglas McKay

Understanding with the Heart[1]

A gift of tongues miracle. Speaking in English; understanding in Spanish.—H.B.L.

In the picturesque chapel in Uruguay, during the double session conference of the Montevideo District on October 4, 1959, more than 1,300 members, investigators, and friends of the Church listened as Elder Harold B. Lee of the Council of the Twelve and his lovely wife, Fern T. Lee, delivered their inspiring messages.

From the early moments of the morning session, evidence of an understanding between the speakers and congregation existed. Sister Lee began with these prayerful words:

> With all my heart I wish I could speak to you in your language this morning. I am so grateful that there is a translator who can interpret my thoughts and feelings to you in your language. I sincerely ask the blessings of our Heavenly Father to be with you and me that we can understand each other's hearts.

Sister Lee's prayer was answered far beyond her own expectations. From the early moments of the first session, both the hearts and feelings of many Uruguayan people were truly in tune with the heartfelt utterances that morning. Even though the interpreter, Elder César Guerra, rendered a commendable translation from the English to the Spanish language, there was no necessity for it as the majority of eager listeners, many with tears of joy in their eyes, comprehended the message. They "understood with their hearts" the words of the Lord's servant as they left his lips.

In Elder Lee's introductory remarks to the people, he had said:

> When we bear our testimonies ... we do not think to do it as so many words, but we speak from our hearts when we declare our faith. Scriptures may be understood, but when a speaker talks by the Spirit of God and an honest person listens to that same Spirit, both are edified together. So I pray this morning that I might speak by that Spirit and you might listen by that Spirit.

All persons in attendance were indeed edified on that memorable October morning. The Spirit bore witness with a meaningful, unforgettable demonstration of love and harmony between the devoted couple from the Salt Lake Valley and the hundreds of happy Uruguayan Saints and visitors. Once again, the Holy Ghost had touched the receptive hearts of honest men and women; the gift of the interpretation of tongues was undeniably present.

Following the conference Elder Lee was surprised to discover that the people who assembled around him for a warm handshake and personal greeting did not understand the English language. "Why, they spoke to me in Spanish!" he exclaimed, "and I was so certain that they knew the English language, for they nodded their heads approvingly during my sermon, even before the translation was rendered!"

The words of the Apostle Paul take on a deeper, far more significant meaning to the Latter-day Saints in Uruguay following Elder Lee's visit:

I will pray with the spirit, and I will pray with the under-standing also: I will sing with the spirit, and I will sing with the understanding also.... In the Church I had rather speak five words with my understanding, that by my voice I might teach other also, than ten thousand words in an unknown tongue. (1 Corinthians 14:15, 19).

Notes

[1]Prepared for publication in *The Church News.*

12

Christine Robinson

Pure Love in Action

With pure love President Lee blesses a good friend and fights for his life with his faith. The patient escapes death to live another 18 years and fulfill a special saving mission of his own.

On April 27, 1972, Dr. O. Preston Robinson, general manager and editor of the Deseret News Publishing Company, suddenly became ill with flu-like symptoms. After his condition worsened, with a fever of 104 degrees, he was admitted to the LDS Hospital on May 1, 1972.

When the Robinsons' son, Bruce, a prominent neuorsurgeon, arrived from Michigan, he broke down at finding his father so desperately ill. As Pres was taken into the intensive care unit, Preston's wife, Christine, remained in his former room to pray on her knees for many hours. Although she was alone, she felt there was someone actually in the room with her and that this personage had come to take her beloved "Pres" away.

In the four or five days of terrific struggle for life, many of the Apostles of the Church came to express concern and to bless Pres, including his brother-in-law, Elder Gordon B. Hinckley, who prayed long and fervently.

Of this ordeal, Christine wrote the following:

> I could not rest, sleep or eat during this period of time and early Saturday morning, when I was on my knees, I felt a great

need to call President Harold B. Lee. I waited until I thought that Brother Lee would be awake and I called him about 7:30 in the morning. He said that he and his wife, Joan, had just arisen from their knees where they had been imploring our Father in Heaven to help Pres and he said that he felt a great urgency, and that he would come to the hospital and be there in about 15 minutes.

Christie Robinson Burton, daughter of Pres and Christine, met President Lee when he arrived. She said later, "I was so impressed with the spirituality and humility of this man. We walked together down the corridor of the hospital, our arms entwined, to see Mother. I felt the great power of his presence and his great love."

When President Lee arrived, he, Bruce, and Christine entered the intensive care section where Pres was lying in a coma. Christine had not previously been in that room because the doctors had asked her not to look at Pres, fearing that she would get upset when she saw him connected to the various pieces of medical equipment and looking so ill. Said Christine:

It did seem that every part of Pres's body was connected to some type of medical equipment. [He], of course, was unconscious, but when President Lee put his hand on Pres's shoulder and said, "Pres, look at me," my husband briefly opened his eyes. I took one of Pres's very swollen hands in mine, and as President Lee prayed, it seemed in reality as if there was a shaft of light that went up from Pres in his bed to our Father in Heaven.

President Lee's prayer was long and I have never had such a feeling of spirituality and closeness to my Father in Heaven as I had at this time. Brother Lee said that he was speaking for the Prophet himself, the only living Prophet of our Father in Heaven on earth at this time. He requested that his prayers go past the angels and to the very foot of the throne of our Father in Heaven himself. President Lee pled for Pres's life. He did not say that his life would be spared in any way. He said that we were to bide by the will of our Father in Heaven. He put Pres's life directly in the hands of our Father in Heaven and prayed that whatever would be done for him in any way whatsoever would be directly in accord with the wishes of our Father in Heaven.

President Lee prayed that our Heavenly Father would personally take over Pres's care and direct it. Our son, Bruce, was then blessed that he would have unusual powers to know what to do at exactly the right time for his father.

After the prayer, not any of us moved for some time because we were all so very affected by this tremendous spiritual outpouring to which we had been witnesses. Then, President Lee took hold of Pres's hand and said to him: "Fight. Fight with everything you have to the last rampart." He instructed Bruce that if he had any feelings whatsoever that anything should be done for his father, to do it immediately and not delay even a second. The doctors had been debating whether or not Pres's condition could stand a tracheotomy. It was at this time that Bruce said, "I feel strongly that we should perform this operation."

President Lee then pushed Bruce and said, "Go, have it done immediately!" This operation took place an hour later. Following this operation, Pres's grave illness began to improve gradually.

Sometime later that morning, I went to my husband's bedside and took hold of his hand. As I stood there looking at him, I was all alone, the curtains were pulled, and I felt like a tremendous mantle then came down out of heaven and completely covered me. I could actually feel this mantle start with my head and cover every bit of my body down to the very tips of my toes. I have never had such a feeling. I felt that it was actually a piece of cloth, or something I could reach out my hand and feel. As it covered me, I had a tremendous peace which entered my soul and a great conviction that I knew, beyond a shadow of a doubt, that Pres's life was going to be spared, that he would have all his faculties, and that he would live and yet do a great work here upon the earth.

Many times after this, I was told by the doctors that Pres would not live, but this did not affect me in any way, because I knew that he would live. The personage, or whoever it was that had been at my side all the time, disappeared and no one could convince me that Pres was not going to live and have his full faculties, despite the fever which reached 106.6, the highest ever seen by this doctor, who said if it were not lowered it would have burned out Pres's brain cells.

* * *

President Lee and President N. Eldon Tanner, both of whom had visited Preston, announced in the Council of the Twelve meeting on May 11 that a miracle had taken place in Pres Robinson's recovery, and it was recorded in the "Modern Acts of the Apostles." President Lee visited twice after he had administered to him, once to give him another blessing.

After his remarkable, rapid, and complete recovery, Pres Robinson wrote to President Harold B. Lee and conveyed his heartfelt appreciation for his "great" expression of "pure love in action."

The fact that you and Joan had just been on your knees praying for me and that you ... responded so unhesitatingly with such love and concern to Christine's telephone call, has further endeared both of you to us and will be remembered forever. Although I did not hear the marvelous administration and blessing that you gave me, both Christine and Bruce have filled me in on a few of the details. They have said that it was the most humble, yet the most powerful and beautiful blessing that either of them had ever heard. We are all convinced that it went straight to the throne of our Father in Heaven, who, through the special keys and gifts you possess, heard and answered positively.

When President Lee recorded in his journal this experience, it was with characteristic humility: "On the following day Pres rallied, talked coherently, seemingly has passed the crisis, and was on his way up—no doubt another miracle of healing, in the Lord's way."

Christie Robinson Burton, daughter of Pres and Christine, said that her father recovered completely from his devastating illness and did not suffer any adverse reactions to his high temperature of 106 degrees. In fact, his vigor and vitality seemed to improve. His mind, which had always been clear, precise, and ever searching, became even stronger. He was even more highly motivated than before. His physical body returned to its previously strong state. He often remarked after twice-yearly physicals, "The doctors say that my heart is like a teenager's!" He was most definitely blessed with a rejuvenation of spirit, mind, and body. There was a profound divine purpose for his more than complete recovery.

For seven or eight years, both Preston and Christine were active in speaking engagements and meeting heads of state throughout the world. Their previous visits to the Mideast, with subsequent interviews with President Hussein of Jordan, and President Nasser of Egypt, were valuable, insightful contributions in a world that was experiencing increasing unrest in these areas.

They both continued to write their memoirs and various articles regarding the Dead Sea Scrolls, and the political difficulties in Lebanon. Pres also completed a monograph on science and religion, "The Breath of Life," which proved to be most thought-provoking and a perfect example of the type of intellect he had always enjoyed.

* * *

Christie Robinson Burton tells the sequel to this story, which gives even greater meaning to the amazing recovery of her father.

Mother contracted Parkinson's disease and severe phlebitis in the early 1980s. Her health began to deteriorate rapidly, compounded by a heart attack. Although she was able to communicate verbally for several years, her body began to waste away and her muscles to atrophy. Hospital stays and physical therapy helped temporarily, but she soon became a complete invalid.

Dad, with his renewed strength and vigor, took over her laborious care. He took her for rides in the wheelchair, and even on trips. He was certain that she would enjoy the winters more in Sun City, Arizona, so he made certain that they made the trek every autumn, coming back to Salt Lake again in the spring.

I remember many times standing out in front of the ladies rest room, guarding the door while Dad was taking care of her personal needs inside. Her care was uppermost in his mind. There came a time when even his energy—he was now in his early 80s—began to diminish, and it was obvious that there needed to be some additional care in the home to protect Dad.

Help came in the form of a choice Hispanic woman named Ramona Haro who was recruited for domestic service. She stayed with Dad and Mom throughout the rest of their lives. She made certain that Dad got good, healthful meals, his clothes were washed, and the house was cleaned. Dad also trained her to help him with Mother, for as she got weaker, it took two people to turn her, to carry her to the wheelchair, etc.

This also freed Dad, so he could get some much-needed exercise. He could now resume playing golf, a sport he loved. Twice a week he was on the course, enjoying the camaraderie of good friends. Soon both his mind and body were invigorated once again.

His care and concern for Mother was beyond reproach. Tenderly and kindly he took care of her, never complaining about his lot in life. The days were often very difficult and lonely. She was unable to communicate with him, and seeing her lie there day after day must have been a sore trial for him. He missed her touch, the warmth of her hand, and the joy of her smile. He couldn't really "get on with his life," for she was there to remind him of his commitment and promise.

As a family, we all assumed that Mother would pass away long before Dad. He had her obituary already written and the burial plot ready in Farmington, Utah.

Amazingly, Dad suffered a heart attack while playing golf on the first of November 1990. He lay in a coma in the St. Mark's hospital for ten days. Despite powerful priesthood blessings, he passed away on November 10, 1990. It was his time to go.

Faithful Ramona Haro continued to take care of my mother, living with her in the home. Mother subsequently passed away on July 2, 1991.

I know in my heart that the miraculous and complete healing of my father, which gave him 18 years of extended life, was for a divine purpose. I was personally and deeply touched by the blessing rendered to my father by President Harold B. Lee, and felt the strong spiritual intervention on my Father's behalf. Dad and Mother were both able to "endure to the end" during very trying and difficult circumstances. Dad's patience, long suffering, tenderness, love unfeigned, and complete devotion to his wife during her long years of illness should serve to be a great example to all of us in our own individual family relationships.

13

C. Berg Jensen

Righteousness Rewarded

A storybook classic World War II tale of survival from enemy attacks, the testimony of a model LDS serviceman, and the life-long blessings that followed.

I was serving a full-time LDS mission in Kelso, Washington, in 1941 when I was drafted into the 41st Division as an infantry private. Two weeks after I was drafted into the U. S. Army, I received my honorable release by letter from President Heber J. Grant.

I was a member of the same 3rd Platoon throughout my Army career. Our outfit landed in Melbourne, Australia, about five months after Pearl Harbor. From Australia we made amphibious landings in Papua New Guinea and Dutch New Guinea; the last two were to the Philippines. By the time we had finished our service, only 10 men were left of the original 48 men in the 3rd Platoon. About one-third were killed, one-third wounded, and one-third hospitalized for malaria and jungle infections. I was hospitalized in combat field hospitals twice for infections.

I was the only Mormon boy in our company, so I was always very conscious of the fact that the Church would be judged by my conduct. Most of the soldiers were usually pretty high from the drinking that went on. After they had had a few drinks they became very persistent in insisting that I have a drink. When they found out I didn't drink, the comments were all about the same. They would say, "I wish I could turn down a drink as easy as you can. You're one in a million. I have yet to see the time you take a drink." I knew I would rather have the respect and friendship of my buddies than all the wealth of the world.

One morning about five o'clock I was one of three in a fox hole. I was sitting up as it was my turn to watch; the other two were trying to sleep. I could hear Japanese soldiers moving and talking in front of our hole. They were getting ready to attack. One enemy soldier, 30 yards in front of us, hollered and said, "Hello there, hello there." I suppose he was trying to get us to answer, so he could locate us. I woke my buddies with "Here they come."

We all listened and stared into the jungle blackness, rifles ready. We could see nothing, but we could hear them talking. They were out of range of grenades, so we waited for one of them to hit a grenade booby trap. I felt in the darkness where I had my grenades stacked to make sure they were handy. We heard a grenade go off, and the enemy gave us heavy machine gun and rifle fire, plus hand grenades. We returned their fire. Rifle bullets were singing past our heads. Grenades were coming toward us trailing fire. Some sailed over our hole. They hit a few feet all around us outside of our fox hole. When a grenade would go off close by, I would drop flat on the ground, grab a grenade, pull the pin, rise to my knee, and let her go.

It is a wonder I didn't get hit by a bullet or piece of grenade. The grenades seemed to be hailing down on us. I thought to myself if they keep tossing grenades, one is bound to hit in our hole. Then, as quick as it started, it stopped. Everything became deathly quiet. One of us said, "Boy, she was kind of hot for a while."

We all laughed, and it relieved the tension.

When we moved out we saw enemy soldiers laying everywhere. Some were so close to us they could have used bayonets.

Once I found myself face-to-face with enemy soldiers among the trees in front of me. I made a mad dash for my fox hole, and then heard several bullets hitting just outside my fox hole.

Another time I saw an enemy grenade trailing smoke heading straight for me in an arch, but it hit a small blackened tree snag just in front of me and exploded a short distance away to my right. Just then a bullet hit in the rocks about three inches from my face, throwing dust and pieces of sharp rock into my right cheek. I searched the area above me and to my front, and saw the enemy soldier who had fired at me. I took careful aim and fired four rapid shots with my M-1 rifle. All was quiet thereafter.

In a battle one morning, I lost my best buddy. I wept in my fox hole that night.

These battlefield stories were included in a letter I wrote to my uncle, Lorenzo Berg, who had been an infantry veteran of World War I. I also wrote that—

> The one who has had the greatest influence on my life for good is my mother. The love of the gospel which she has instilled in me by the things she said and did has helped me more than anything else to withstand the many temptations there are in the Army.
>
> There is nothing more certain to me than that God lives and answers prayers and that Jesus is the Christ, the Son of God. Never before have I felt the need of the protection of my Heavenly Father as I have here. It has been while lying in a fox hole in mud and water that I have really felt the nearness of God. At times I felt like I could almost reach out and touch Him. Many have felt the same way.
>
> I know that as long as I or anyone else keep the commandments of God, none of Satan's stratagems will be able to break through the armor of righteousness which fortifies us against sin. Once we cease living righteously we lose the Spirit of God and we are headed for unhappiness and destruction. The only ones who know true happiness are those who conform their lives to the teachings of our Lord and Savior.
>
> Some people will say that I've just been lucky, that the

Lord had nothing to do with the fact that I am alive today. No one knows better than I do that the reason I am alive today is because the Lord has seen fit to preserve my life until my allotted time on Earth is finished. If it is God's will, I will live to see my loved ones again and be married and raise a family.

Regardless of what I have gone through or the suffering I may endure before this conflict culminates in peace, I will have no complaints, because I know it will be sanctified to my good. There is only one thing lacking in my life to make it complete and happy, and that is a wife. With the help of the Lord I will find the kind of a girl I want to be my wife.

In my South Pacific outfit we used to accuse each other in a jovial way, that we would probably marry the first girl we met when we got back to the States. When I was discharged my folks were supposed to come into Great Falls, Montana, to pick me up early on a Sunday morning. But I arrived earlier than scheduled, so I decided to hitchhike the 20 miles to our home. When I arrived at our home I went into the house and found everything very quiet. I decided my folks had already gone into town to pick me up, so I looked around to see if anyone was at home, but found no one.

I went to the basement where I noticed a girl sleeping in a bed. I thought she must have been one of my sisters so I went over and sat on the edge of the bed, thinking she would awaken and tell me which sister she was. She didn't move.

I went back upstairs and there was my dad and mother with two of my sisters. After we exchanged hugs and kisses, I asked, "Who is that girl downstairs in bed?" My older sister went downstairs and in a few minutes returned with a beautiful girl who took my breath away. "This is my very good friend, Betty Blackburn," she said.

Betty was the first girl I met after returning from 39 months overseas. After a short engagement, we were married for time and all eternity in the Idaho Falls Temple.

We have been blessed with five sons and two daughters. All five of our sons have filled full-time missions and attended BYU; three have graduated. Four sons have been married in temples. Our oldest daughter was married in the Salt Lake Temple and graduated from BYU. Our youngest daughter, a graduate of Ricks College, was also married in the temple. We have 20 grandchildren and looking forward now to great-grandchildren.

I had wonderful parents who loved each other dearly. I know I was born of "goodly parents." We were blessed to have been raised on a farm. We did not work on Sunday, except for doing the daily chores. Mother always emphasized the importance of prayer. Dad emphasized the importance of work. It is an unbeatable combination. We knelt around the kitchen table every night and morning for family prayers.

I am grateful that my life was spared in those viciously fought battles in the Pacific 50 years ago to allow the glorious blessings which have filled my adult life in the Church and with my wonderful family. God has been so good to me.

David O. McKay

Victor C. Hancock

A Convert's Dream

Miracles of Elder Lee's 1959 tour of the Central American Mission included the healing of a blind boy and a remarkable dream.

After Elder Harold B. Lee visited the Central American Mission in November 1959, President Victor C. Hancock[1] wrote in his mission report, "that mission has not been the same since that time. The inspiration of the Lord has come upon those people." President Hancock also made note of Elder Lee's comment that they were to have leaders from among the 1,595 people gathered to hear Elder Lee speak.

According to President Hancock's report, Elder Lee gave a blessing to a small boy whose eyesight was steadily decreasing to the point that he was nearly blind. When President Hancock visited the branch some time later, a little boy stood up and bore his testimony. President Hancock did not recognize the boy until someone said, "That is the boy that received the blessing from Brother Lee." Said President Hancock of this miraculous transformation, "He did not have to have any aid. He did not need anyone to lead him around."

President Hancock's report also made reference to a remarkable dream that came to a full-blooded Indian, Daniel Mich, who would later become a leader in the Patzicía Branch. Brother Mich told of a dream he had had before joining the Church. Seven men, he said, were beckoning him to follow them, each on a different road. Daniel had just been visited by the missionaries, and despite the vicious stories being told about the Church, he had been praying to know the truth of their message. In his dream he saw a tall, stately, white-haired man who introduced himself as David O. McKay, a prophet of God, who told him the way to the right road. Later, when the Elders showed him a picture of President McKay, Daniel immediately recognized him as the prophet of his dream. He was baptized not long afterwards.

As Elder Lee met with nearly 1,600 members from the five districts of Guatemala he described his "strong feeling that this place is without question the Lamanite capital of North America and that a temple for the Latin American people should be built here." This nonpublished prophecy was fulfilled in 1981 when President Spencer W. Kimball announced temple construction plans for Guatemala on the day before the opening of April general conference.

Notes

[1] President Hancock passed away in July 1987.

15

David S. King

A Miracle Birth into a Family of Love

A talented surgeon and a blessing from Elder Lee save the last pregnancy of a mother threatened by a tumor.

In the fall of 1956 Elder Lee administered to Rosalie King, whose pregnancy was jeopardized by the presence of a suspected tumor. About a week following this Rosalie felt serious abdominal pains and cramping. Immediate surgery was indicated. Twenty-four hours later, a nonmalignant tumor the size of a small grapefruit was removed from her uterus. Rosalie and her husband David felt most fortunate in securing the services a physician of exceptional ability, as well as of deep spirituality.

After the operation was over, the couple learned that the chances of Rosalie's having retained her pregnancy through an operation of such magnitude and severity, in the light of her previous medical history, had been extremely remote. Moreover, had the crisis which created the necessity for the operation occurred sooner, or later, than it did, the pregnancy would have been almost certainly lost. Yet, it was preserved.

After the birth of the baby, who was named Matthew Thomas King, David King wrote to Elder Lee, thanking him again for his blessing. To this, Elder Lee wrote, "I can see now what you meant by telling me about the Lord's help in providing you with the family you now have. I am grateful that you gave me the opportunity of being a party in helping you through the last difficult period. Please give my love to your wife."

* * *

Of his son Matthew, David King said 36 years later, "He was with us when I served as United States Ambassador to the Malagasy Republic. He therefore was able to learn French fluently as a boy of ten years. He later served very successfully in the French-Belgian Mission, using to excellent advantage the French language skills he had acquired in Madagascar."

Matthew graduated from Brigham Young University with a masters degree in business administration. He was sealed for time and eternity to a wonderful returned sister missionary, Laurie Bell. The young couple became the parents of six children. "Their home is a pure delight to visit," said David King. "They have the usual problems which every couple rearing a large family faces. No one is exempt. But they have been able to cope, and, in my opinion, do so quite successfully."

Matthew has served in several ward positions, and also as an active stake missionary and temple ordinance worker. "Matthew and his wife have been one of the great inspirations of my life," continued David. "He has been able to feed me spiritually as well as intellectually, and I consider every moment I spend with him, or with his wife and family, to be a pure gift from Heaven. I have no doubt that Matthew was specially called to come to earth when he did, and that the Lord loves him in that special way reserved for those who serve him with particular devotion.

"I have other children, now long-since grown to full maturity, whom I love with equal intensity. Were I to talk about them, I would give an equally enthusiastic account. They are all different, but are all very much loved. Our extended family is a family of love."

David King later related the following vignette about President Harold B. Lee. When David was bishop of the Kensington Ward (1971-1978), a sister bore her testimony at a fast and testimony meeting, and described how her small son had been born with a body tragically deficient. It had to do with the internal structure of his intestines—most of them missing—and he had only been sustained in life by a series of painful operations. As he grew in size, these operations had to be repeated.

On this occasion, he was ready for a further operation; however, his mother had been told that if he was operated upon, he had a 50-50 chance of surviving. If he was not operated, he had a 100% chance of not surviving.

This sister, in bearing her testimony, said that she had talked with President Lee over the phone, and told him about her plight. (President Lee often insisted on taking such calls when he could.) In her testimony she said President Lee had been so moved by her suffering that he told her that he would join her in fasting for the success of that operation. What makes the story so poignant is that President Lee, himself, died only a few days thereafter.

Brother King said he wept when he heard the story of this mother. "In our experience," said Brother King, "we found President Lee to be a very concerned and deeply loving individual. We remember him fondly for his intimate service to our family."

16

H. Alton Johnson

A Spiritual Transfusion

A World War II story where the spirit of his son-in-law, Hall, then in fierce battle in Italy, came so powerfully upon him that he knew he needed special help. That day was the very day that Hall received near fatal wounds.

In 1941 our oldest daughter, Twila, married Sergeant Hall Bingham in the Salt Lake Temple. After a year of her following him from one place to another, he was sent overseas to Africa. Hall went through the war there, then to the Anzio beachhead and the horrors there.

It was on the eleventh day of May, 1941, as I was going to my work at Twin Falls, Idaho from Jerome, about noon, that I was driving along and it seemed as if Hall, who was somewhere in Italy, was sitting beside me on the seat. His presence was so much there that it startled me. It impressed me so much that I stopped at the side of the road, took off my hat, and prayed to the Lord to give Hall strength to overcome anything that might be wrong with him and to return him safely to his wife and little child. After I prayed I was so weak that I couldn't lift my arms to the steering wheel, and I remained in this condition for several minutes. For the rest of the day, I kept this prayer in my heart.

That evening as I returned home, the fear was lifted from my heart and I sang hymns all the way. I asked my wife to have Twila write and ask Hall just what happened on that day, which she did.

We did not receive any answer to the letter, but a few days later we received a telegram saying Hall was seriously wounded and that we would be kept informed concerning his condition. It was two weeks later before additional word was received from a Red Cross nurse telling us Hall was improving. About 30 days later another letter came informing our daughter that Hall was in a hospital in Walla Walla, Washington. She was forbidden to come to see him until another ten days passed. When she visited him, she found Hall with both arms and both legs shot almost beyond repair, in addition to numerous body wounds.

She was able to check his mail to learn where he had been on the day I had prayed for him. She discovered that just four days before that day, Hall had led his company out on the great push toward Rome. His battalion had gone quite some distance into enemy territory, and those who were left had been surrounded while trying to work their way back.

Hall had stepped on a land mine, which accounted for most of his injuries and had lain unattended for four days and nights. He watched as his buddies were killed by enemy fire or died slowly of extensive wounds. Then he said to the one soldier left, "We either get out of here now or never."

Hall had been praying every moment that he had been conscious. He said about this time he found himself strong enough that he could crawl, first by using his forehead, then his chin on the ground, to pull himself along. The medics picked him up in the evening of that day.

God had answered my prayer. Hall has almost completely recovered although he is considered almost totally disabled by the U. S. Government. Nevertheless, he was able to work in the laboratory at the Jerome Co-op Creamery and raise four children. Hall currently has fifteen grandchildren and four great-grandchildren. The baby girl Hall came home to, grew up, married in the temple, and blessed Hall and his wife with five of their grandchildren, three of whom served missions.

17

"God has provided a means that man...might work mighty miracles."

Mosiah 8:18

E.D.B.

A Blessing Dictated from Heaven

In a successful maternity blessing the words were divinely uttered and others, unseen, were also in the room.—H.B.L.

After my husband and I had two children, a boy and a girl, we lost four babies in a row. We prayed and sought the advice of several physicians. One said not to even try to have any more children, as they probably would die before birth. If they were lucky enough to be born, he added, they would be abnormal in some way. Both my husband and I were heartbroken.

In the early part of June 1954, I decided to seek advice from Elder Harold B. Lee. He kindly offered to give me a blessing with the aid of Brother John Longdon. It was wonderful, and as he began to speak I heard the words twice, one word and then the same word, like the echo of a public address system. I thrilled to think what might be the reason for this, and yet at the same time I wondered if Brother Longdon was simply repeating the words after Elder Lee.

The following May 6, 1955, we were blessed with a beautiful little baby girl. The doctors anticipated the worst and had everything ready for a transfusion, but it was not necessary. She was perfectly beautiful in every way. One doctor remarked how lucky I was, but I know it was not luck, but the blessing of our dear Heavenly Father.

At the time of the blessing, my heart was so full that I did not tell him how I had heard the words of the blessing twice. In June, when I brought my children to see Elder Lee, I asked him about it. I shall never forget his words, for they verified my own feelings. He said: "We three were not alone in the room."

I wish everyone in the Church could feel the welling up within me, at the knowledge that I had been so blessed, for I knew without a shadow of a doubt we have a living, loving Heavenly Father, and his son, Jesus Christ, is our Savior.

*Initials only used at author's request.

18

Richard W. Madsen III

Lifted from the Grave

This father of five young children, apparently doomed by a fatal blood disorder, was saved from the grave by the blessing of four apostles, and was granted 24 additional years of life.

In 1960 a friend asked me to be a blood donor for an infant relative of his from Idaho, a little boy who was to undergo heart surgery. As I had been a successful blood donor as recently as seven months prior to this invitation and on 33 previous occasions, I accepted without hesitation and made an appointment for the blood-drawing at the LDS Hospital in Salt Lake City for the following day.

As I recollect, I had been feeling very irritable, tired and faint for possibly two months prior to this date. But I had blamed my lack of vigor to my busy Christmas schedule at the furniture store where I was employed, which annually brought on physical exhaustion and extreme nervousness.

At the blood center in the hospital I filled out the customary personal health history-card, had my blood pressure checked, my heart-beat audited, and then had a drop of blood drawn from a finger tip by pricking the skin. The nurse's face gave me the first inkling that something was amiss.

She looked gravely at me for a moment, as if pre-packaging her thought in careful words, then said: "You're not going to give anyone a transfusion, Mr. Madsen; in fact, before you leave this hospital, you should arrange to have a complete physical, with a blood study and X-rays of your abdomen. You are extremely anemic, and my guess is that you are hemorrhaging internally. It is surprising that you haven't had lapses into unconsciousness!"

She summoned a doctor from the laboratory nearby on the same floor. After an exchange of words, he approached me.

"I'd like to draw a larger blood specimen for study," he said. "I'd also like to speak with your doctor and apprise him of the results." When he asked for my doctor's name, I gave him my brother-in-law's name, as he was my doctor. I could see that the doctor standing before me recognized my doctor's name, who was also a noted obstetrician in this area, hardly a doctor for a middle-aged man, he was no doubt thinking!

I disregarded the suggestion that I remain in the waiting room and returned to the store where I continued normal activity through the day.

That evening I received a telephone call from my doctor setting up an appointment for me to receive a physical examination from an associate of his.

This examination took most of the following afternoon. It included various specimens of body fluids, examination of the body cavities, and X-ray pictures. He also checked my heart beat, blood pressure, and nervous reactions, then drew more blood for study and the compilation of a rather all-inclusive personal history.

I was told that my eyes were good, my ears were good, my heart was good, my teeth were good, my reflexes were good, my lungs were good, my blood pressure was good, and that there was no indication of internal hemorrhage.

He concluded by saying that, except for my blood, I was in good health. My blood count, both for red and for white cells, was dangerously low, however, and indicated something drastically was wrong, possibly a blood cancer, such as leukemia, which was destroying the red cells as they were produced, or a plastic anemia, a failure of the marrow and glands to produce the cells initially. Either, he said blandly, was probably fatal.

The doctor gave me a special diet, jars full of iron pills and preparations, and told me to get lots of sleep, go out for a walk out-of-doors daily, and "not to worry."

"Aplastic anemia," he said, "can be brought on through poisoning from such sources as histaminic drugs to which one might become sensitized." He pointed out that Dristan was an offender with some people and seemed pleased to hear that I had used a quantity of this medication just about a month prior to the discovery of my ailment. Caught soon enough, the failure of the marrow to produce cells might be righted though restoration was slow and doubtful, at best.

I didn't want to frighten my family, or my parents, by dramatically announcing my impending funeral, but my concern was obvious. Steadfastly, my family refused to panic. They met me with cheerful smiles and encouragement, and I reciprocated as brightly as I could. But the pretense was not convincing, and we all had a sense of finality. Prayer was our only avenue of hope, and pray we did.

After two weeks had passed, the test results were in. However, they were inconclusive. More blood was drawn, more tests were taken, more questions were asked. "What medicine have you taken in the past two years? Think hard, is that all? What about aspirin? Don't leave out a thing. Do you remember being around paint, varnish, lacquer, paint thinner in the past two years? Which ones? When? How frequently?"

In the meantime I ate liver, I walked, I took iron tablets, I tried to sleep and I worried. I prepared my will. I looked at my wife and children, even fellow employees, as if each look might be my last. I read their concern and their pity in their eyes. I was a condemned man and no one could do a thing.

Few can know the abject despair and self-pity one can feel as he looks at his sweet children—all under age fourteen—suddenly made quiet, unsmiling, and apprehensive as they try to comprehend that their father, standing there as always, will soon be no more; nor can he look at this wife, smiling loyally and feigning confidence she doesn't feel, as she contemplates widowhood with five young children yet to raise and educate.

"Why me?" I asked myself. "This couldn't be happening to me. I'm watching a plot develop in a play or a book. Surely I won't die! Not me! I'm only thirty-nine. My family needs me. I've always been big, strong and healthy; someone's made an awful mistake!"

But I could sense an ebbing of vitality from day-to-day. My ears rang; my eyes saw dancing polka dots day and night; I wanted to sit down rather than stand up, to lie down rather than sit, to sleep rather than think. When I walked daily, it was sheer torture. Each time I wondered if I would make it back under my own power. My ears, hands, and feet felt cold and clammy. I felt comfortable only when reclining in a hot bath.

Yes, the doctors were right. There was something drastically wrong. I felt that the seeds of death had been planted and were even now growing hourly ... in spite of my family, in spite of our prayers, and in spite of myself!

What should a condemned man do with his final hours? Work as usual, meditate and pray, vacation with the family, make love (which I wasn't physically capable of doing, anyway), write his memoirs, work in the temple, rush to the Mayo Clinic? It didn't matter, really. I kept working, kept praying, kept hoping, kept worrying.

As I was writing an ad at work one day, my brother-in-law called me and said that I was to be admitted to the hospital for a bone biopsy and further study in just two hour's time. Everything had been arranged quietly without my knowledge.

The blood tests showed a continued decline. The situation was now desperate, calling for immediate last-ditch efforts to find a cause and develop a cure.

During the next two hours I resigned myself to death. I had a few requests and suggestions for my children, privately and together. I told my wife and my mother of my insurance, my debts, my lock-box, my will, and my hopes for the family.

My father rushed from the store, and together my parents, my wife, and I rode to the hospital in his car, none of us knowing what to say or how to say it.

My mother told me that Elder Harold B. Lee of the Quorum of the Twelve had responded to her request and would come to the hospital and administer to me. He was in the regular weekly quorum meeting in the temple and would be up late in the afternoon. How grateful I felt and yet how embarrassed that I should occasion a disruption in his busy schedule. Everything hinged on the Lord, and on His intervention. How I prayed that Elder Lee would promise me a recovery! That and only that would right my bodily functions and permit me an extension of my mortal probation.

But I wondered, should I, should he, should we, importune the Lord to change the course of events? If I am to die, is there not good and sufficient reason for it? I wanted to live; but would I rather live than be obedient to the plans of the Lord? Was I ready to die? Surely I had not measured up to my opportunities, had not been as valiant as my testimony urged me to be nor as unworthy as my conscience would have me be. True, I'd never tasted alcohol, tobacco, tea or coffee; and true, I was a tithe payer. I was sure God lived and the Church was true and divine, that this mortality was part of His overall plan and that life is eternal and death was but a door through which we must all pass. I knew there was no promotion without change, and that death could be graduation, progress, new challenge and opportunity.

"But I can't die and leave my family!" I thought. "I can't face the Lord! I'm not ready. I haven't been a productive steward of the opportunities the Lord has given me." Oh yes, I tried hard on my mission and I had the Spirit of the Lord with me. I know His power. I knew the feeling of constant guidance and inspiration, of fearlessness and of burning desire to shout from the housetops that Jesus is the Christ, and His Church is on the earth, restored to furnish saving guidance and ordinances for His children everywhere. The fever of testimony had burned brightly within me; I had thrilled to the core with the knowledge that the gospel was literally true and unspeakably wonderful! That feeling had never left me.

At the hospital, I was given a blood pressure test, and specimens of urine and blood were taken for study. I went upstairs to my room, and sat there, fully dressed, talking to my family. Almost at once, Elder Lee arrived, accompanied by Elders Kimball, Petersen and Stapley! One third of the Quorum of the Twelve on the earth were there in my room!

In response to their request for a preference, I asked Elder Kimball to anoint and Elder Lee to seal the blessing.

That room became transformed to an outpost of God's heaven! The world and worldliness drained away! The voice, the united hands, the supplication of these "special witnesses" of the Savior, went straight to the throne of the Lord. I knew that my life and my well-being were being decided in sacred conversation at that moment. Should I live? Should I die? What was God's will?

I knew it as Brother Lee intoned it, "You will recover. You will live. The angel of death will pass you by." His prayer had begun in quest of divine guidance, and now he declared the decision to me, cautioning me to redouble my efforts in behalf of the Lord, the giver of all blessings. Tears streamed down my cheeks and for the first time in weeks, I smiled because I felt relieved, confident, happy and glad to be alive!

That evening were interviews, more pills, more blood-pressure checks, then shaving, disinfecting, and bandaging of the hip area for the bone biopsy in the morning for a study of the marrow. Another drawing of blood for analysis showed that my blood tested higher for the first time.

The next morning I was awakened in the morning preparatory to surgery, and another blood test was made. I then was given drugs to start me on the way to unconsciousness. The operation proved the point. My marrow was newly alive with healthy, young red corpuscles. I was still on thin ice, but on the road to recovery.

Just prior to my hospitalization, my blood count had been very low, virtually unchanged from the previous month when it was discovered that my marrow was not producing sufficient blood cells to sustain me. Even after the bone marrow biopsy (and the accompanying cessation of eating, pill-taking, etc.), my blood cells did an amazing thing: the cell count nearly doubled overnight!

The report from the laboratory technicians was equally indicative of the intervention of the Lord. While the outer perimeter of the bone section was filled with inactive, depressed marrow and dead cells, the inner recesses were vibrant with vigorous, perfectly normal marrow of fresh origin and with a great swarm of young blood cells. The doctors predicted that within three weeks my condition would be normal. There was no remaining sign of leukemia or of a plastic anemia." "A miracle," said the doctor. "I've never seen anything like it," chorused the laboratory technicians, the interns, and the nurses.

It is marvelous to contemplate the power of the priesthood which the Lord has placed amongst men ... the great vitality of faith. How blessed we all are that the immense knowledge and strength of our Creator is responsive to our needs.

With a full heart, I thank the Lord for my life, for my family, for the Church, for the priesthood, and for my deep assurance that the restored gospel is God's plan for man's salvation. I am grateful for the opportunities afforded me to develop here in mortality, for nearly four years in the mission field, for nearly two war-time years as a chaplain trainee, for over six years as a guide-missionary on Temple Square. The Lord has been lavish with His blessings. I have been too stinting in my service and appreciation.

For reasons that no doubt are good and sufficient, because they are His, the Lord has commanded that we acknowledge His hand in all things.

I am sure that He didn't intend that one should rent a public hall, buy advertising space, or otherwise publish to the world that which is private, personal and sacred. But He did want us to be humble, to be grateful for His blessings, and to be constantly reminded to live the eternal laws upon which His blessings are predicated.

Probably, also, He knew that some are dependent upon testimony of Divine manifestations in mortal lives to accept the unseen and to bolster quavering faith. Not all can rationalize an understanding of eternal actuality nor be gifted with the testimony of the Spirit. Some need the crutch of reassurance from others who have been blessed with extraordinary experiences.

Nonetheless, in the deepest of humility and with a heart joyous with gratitude, I intend herewith to acknowledge the hand of God in my life, declaring to those who may subsequently be invited to read this experience that the Lord was my physician, faith was the medication, and the power of the priesthood made me well, and, as surely as if it had lifted me from the grave, saved my life.

* * *

Richard's wife, Ruth Lee Madsen, wrote the following:

> For 24 years Dick enjoyed relatively good health and our family rejoiced in having a father to love and nourish us, and teach our young children until they were in their mature years.
>
> He became seriously ill in April 1984 and was diagnosed as having Harry Cell Leukemia in 1985. He died at the age of 63 on January 22, 1985.
>
> There is no way I can express the wonderful blessing of the nearly quarter of a century extension of his life and what it has meant to his loving family and friends. Our gratitude knows no bounds.

19

Doris Hadden

Opening the Door for Family Exaltation

This husband, at a stake conference where his wife was a speaker, gained the strength to stop smoking by contact with the General Authority.—H.B.L.

I had been assigned to speak at our stake conference at LaGrande, Oregon, on February 4-5, 1956. I had to talk at the Saturday night meeting and was very frightened until Elder Harold B. Lee, who was the visiting authority, put me at ease, saying he would pray for me if I prayed for him.

My husband, Bill, and I were a little late in getting to the morning session so we sat in the choir seats, which were very near to where Elder Lee was sitting. I didn't know it at the time, but on the way home that afternoon Bill told me that while he sat there, even before Elder Lee spoke, a queer feeling came over him (one he couldn't explain into words) as if some contact between this special man and him had just taken place. He didn't know what it was. Just then, the thought came to him if he would just try once more to overcome his tobacco habit, that he could do it and not have any more trouble.

Now, my husband and I had prayed very hard about his smoking, and he had been trying to quit for quite a long period of time. For nearly two years he had tried in earnest to quit, knowing how much it meant to me and the children, besides his own desires, for that was the only thing keeping him from being advanced in the priesthood. (Bill was just a deacon when we started back to Church.)

From that Sunday conference with Elder Lee on, he never smoked another cigarette—and the craving and desires from before were all erased from him. It was truly an answer to prayers and a very special blessing to us.

Not long after this, Bill was ordained an elder in LaGrande at leadership meeting, and we went to the Idaho Falls Temple to be married and have our children sealed to us. Our children were surely proud of their daddy. We had wanted to do this more than anything for over three years. With the help of the Lord and Elder Lee, it was at last made possible.

Bill was also set apart as Deacon's Quorum Advisor, where he served as a teacher and enjoyed it very much. When we retired we left Pilot Rock and went to St. George, Utah, for the winters to do temple work and genealogy. We also spent eighteen months in wonderful service at Nauvoo, Illinois, on a mission for the Church from 1991-1993. We have tried to show our thanks by the work we're doing in this part of the Lord's vineyard.

Our lives have been a dream come true. We very much enjoy our blessings from living the gospel and the happiness it has brought to us, since that Sunday 38 years ago when our lives were changed by the influence of Apostle Harold B. Lee.

20

*"Lay your hands
upon the sick, and they
shall recover."*

D&C 66:9

Honolulu, Hawaii—UP, February 8, 1944

Commanded to Remain Alive

*A reporter tells the story of a Priesthood administration involving
two wounded Marines in Kwajulane, South Pacific, in 1944.—
H.B.L.*

Some folks say that the day of miracles has passed. Some people say that things such as this just don't happen, yet here's a story which will leave you breathless and wondering—for it concerns two inconspicuous boys of the United States Marine Corps and the battle for the Marshall Islands.

The time was just before dawn when the great gray hulks which were battleships lay against the cool horizon of the blue Pacific. Aboard those ships, the boys were anxiously awaiting the first signal which would announce the start of the drive to take one of the greatest of Japanese bases, Kwajulane atoll.

Nearer, inshore, yet other boats lay in the silence of the dawn—smaller boats containing the United States Marines. Where the duties of the men aboard the big ships would require the rather remote but strenuous work of bombardment, it was the men on the smaller boats inshore who must wade through the final stretch of water and brave the withering fire of murderous Japanese machine guns.

Slowly the minutes ticked by into what seemed hours. Actually the time was 20 minutes to six, when the final word came. From over the horizon tons of shells began pouring into the Jap positions from the big ships off-shore. It seemed that all Hell broke loose, for the Kwajulane began to heave and surge with a convulsive shock of death. A starflare lit the sky and the smaller boats began pouring out the men who were destined to take the island.

From far above, barely audible at first, then building into a roaring crescendo, allied dive bombers dove toward that small patch of earth, their bombs tearing great holes in the ground and blowing adjacent buildings to bits.

And slowly toward shore, the men of the United States Marines edged closer and closer. In a moment, they would be sighted by the Japanese. In a moment, bullets would begin splattering around them, from pillboxes skillfully hidden on the beach. But on they came—and soon the battle was joined by the men whose glory is destined to be written in the annals of history.

The splatter of machine guns soon lay a death pattern on the men wading toward shore. Here and there, they went down, some wounded, some dead—and it is about two of these wounded that we speak at the moment. The battle went on, and the men of the Marine Corps—despite the wounds and death of their comrades—went in.

Being a war correspondent, my boat was going in behind the first line of men, and we came upon these two, wounded Marines in the water. One from the stain of red around him we could tell was wounded badly. The other, wounded too, was holding the other's head above water.

We picked them up, midst a hail of shots from shore, then pulled back toward safer retreat to render first aid. The one seemed too far gone to need much help, but the other refused aid until his wounded buddy was attended. But our help seemed insufficient, as we soon realized, and we announced our decision to his comrade. Then it happened.

This young man, the better of the two, bronzed by the tropical sun, clean as a shark's tooth in the South Seas, slowly got to his knees. His one arm was gone, but with the other, he lifted the head of his unconscious pal into his lap, placed his good hand on the other's pale brow and uttered what to us seemed to be incredible words—words which to this moment are emblazoned in unforgettable letters across the doorway of my memory:

"In the name of Jesus Christ, and by virtue of the holy priesthood which I hold, I command you to remain alive until the necessary help can be obtained to secure the preservation of your life."

Today the three of us are here in Honolulu and he is still alive. In fact, we walked down the beach together today, as we convalesce. He is the wonder of the medical unit, for—they say—he should be dead. Why he isn't they don't know—but we do, for we were there, off the shores of Kwajulane.

21

H. Burke Peterson

Converted by Televised Conference

A Salt Lake nonmember watched the televised opening address of President Lee at the April 1973 General Conference, which led to his conversion and baptism.

When I was serving as a Regional Representative in November 1971, I was assigned one weekend to a stake conference in Mesa. Then I received a telephone call from President Lee's office asking if I could accompany President Lee to one of the stake conferences in Phoenix. (It was the stake over which I had one time presided as a stake president.)

Of course, I changed my plans and rather than going to the conference to which I had previously been assigned, I accompanied President Lee to his conference. I wasn't sure why he wanted me to come; he didn't make much of a fuss over my being there. As far as I could determine the visit was totally irrelevant to anything I would consider very important to an inquiry from a member of the First Presidency.

During the Saturday evening meeting he had me say a few words. Then, following the meeting, he asked me to step back in the choir loft to visit with him for a few moments. He talked about my work and my family, and matters such as that, and then he thanked me very much and said, "We'll see you in the morning."

Well, I went home Saturday night and told Brookie, my wife,

that I had just been interviewed. I knew enough about interviewing to know that you don't have to ask certain questions as much as you have to be in tune with the Spirit to find out what you need to find out. "President Lee didn't say he was interviewing me," I told her, "but I just know he was, and I don't know what it was all about." And being the natural man that I am, I immediately began to worry about it.

Sunday morning, after what was a sleepless night for me, President Lee called on me to speak again during the general session of stake conference. Now I've spoken enough to know when I've hit the nail on the head, or when I've missed it completely; and I knew when I sat down that I had really messed up. I felt terrible. I felt like I didn't have the Spirit. I felt like I hadn't given anything to the Saints. I felt just totally deflated.

After the session President Lee shook my hand and thanked me for coming. He didn't make any comment about whether or not my talk was worthwhile, but he said only how much he had appreciated being with me, and that was the end of our visit.

It wasn't until the next spring, March 1972, that I received a phone call at my home from the First Presidency, and President Lee and President N. Eldon Tanner were on the other end of the line. It was then that they extended a call to me to serve in the Presiding Bishopric along with Victor L. Brown and Vaughn J. Featherstone. President Lee mentioned that they were calling in behalf of President Joseph Fielding Smith. That was quite a blow; however, not one that entirely surprised me.

In the second or third meeting the newly called Presiding Bishopric had with the First Presidency in their regular Friday morning setting, President Lee, speaking for the First Presidency, gave us a charge concerning our responsibilities. He then looked at me and said, "I want you to know that your call as First Counselor in the Presiding Bishopric was inspired. Don't you ever forget it." He then continued:

When we called Victor Brown to be the Presiding Bishop

we did not give him any suggestions for counselors, but we
knew that you would be one of them. And when he brought
his recommendations for counselors to us and you were one of
his recommendations, that confirmed what we already knew
the Lord had in mind for you to do.

That was naturally a very comforting realization for me to
remember over the years I served in the Bishopric, and during
some of the trying experiences we always have in those offices
and callings.

President Lee was my hero. He was one of the most remarkable men I've ever met in any leadership position, and he treated
me just royally all the time.

* * *

On June 6, 1973, Bishop H. Burke Peterson wrote to President
Lee to tell him a conversion story told at a session of the Sugar
House Salt Lake Stake conference he had attended. The man had
lived in Salt Lake for eighteen years, having never paid any particular attention to the Church's televised conference broadcast.

However, in April 1973, this man decided to listen because, as
he said, there was "nothing else better being offered." Impressed by
the opening session and President Lee's message, the man hung on
every word that was given from the pulpit for the next three days.

After the conference was concluded, he started to pray out
loud and soon he realized that he was starting to love others as
himself. He inquired of some friends about missionaries, and
after their first lesson he went to his kitchen cabinet and poured
five gallons of whiskey, that he had thought he needed as a good
supply, down the drain. He wasn't an alcoholic, but this had been
a part of his life, just like having bread in the cupboard or milk
in the refrigerator.

In his letter to President Lee, Bishop Peterson described this
man as a being in his mid-forties and "a substantial businessman
in the Salt Lake City community" and then concluded:

He was baptized in the Church on May 19 of this year. He bore as strong and sweet a testimony as I have ever heard of the divinity of the Church and the reality of the Savior.

If this was the only good that came from the April Conference it would have been worth it.... However, I know, and you know, that this story will be repeated many times.

22

Mariella and Rita Colombo

The Miracle of Conversion[1]

> *Two Italian teenage sisters find the Church through the mission-*
> *aries, and yearn for the baptism their parents will not allow.*
> *President Lee comforts them and gives counsel to those who find*
> *the truth but must await its full possession.*

In the late summer of 1973, President Lee received the following letter from two young Italian sisters who wished to be
baptized:

Our loved President:
    We wish to write this letter ... because you are our dear
friend. We had decided to do this a long time ago, but we had
never the courage, and today we have finally done it. You can
help us, and we ask you to listen to us.
    We are two Italian girls. Our names are Mariella and Rita.
We are almost 17 years old, and we are sisters.... Our family is
Catholic, and as far back as one and a half years ago, we were,
too.... Six years ago, when our father, being a medical doctor,
was transferred to Livorno (Tuscany), we were without
friends.... In spite of the company of our brothers and sisters,
we felt terribly alone and sad. But soon, in the apartment
above ours, some Mormon missionaries came to live. We
became acquainted with them and they became our greatest
friends....

The two sisters described how the missionaries had befriended them and taught them, but then had moved. They had no further contact with the Mormons for six years. Then, one day at school, the sisters found a newspaper on one of their desks at school.

Rita started to turn the pages of that newspaper, and her eyes rested on a few big words, which read "SIX MORMONS PREACH..." She lifted her eyes towards me. Her eyes were shining with happiness and a tear was wetting her face; she closed the newspaper and embraced me ... saying, "Jesus loves us a lot!"

We decided to go to Church.... We were very afraid, and this moved us to pray a lot, as we had never done before.... Our fear ended at Church and a great joy filled our hearts....

Soon we learned to pray with our hearts and lips, and the air we were breathing was filled with the spirit of faith and love.... The Lord had spoken to us, and his answer was "Yes"!

... It was so that we met the Church, and we have started to love it and God, the true God.... This has been just our testimony and story. We hope we have not bothered you with it.... We would like to cry out loud to the world what God has given us. We would like to offer all our lives to thank Him for the great blessing He has sent to us.

We have only one very beautiful desire which seems impossible to come true. We want to be baptized. Oh, very dear friend, you don't know how not being baptized burns inside us....

At school, at home, everywhere, we've gotten into trouble just because we have spoken about the Church. Oh, President, we love the Church more than ourselves. We are living for it, and we want to be baptized, but we don't have our parents' permission. We have to wait until we are 21 years old. Five years is a long time, an eternity. It is difficult to wait because our love for the Church and our desire for God is strong. In five years many things may happen. We are afraid, because there are many wicked people. And, also, there is much hatred in the world.

President, we ask your help. Make it possible that we may be baptized soon. Pray for us. We cannot live away from the Church. Tell this to Jesus....

Our parents take us away from God. They condemn us for what we do. Everybody considers us crazy just because we bring God with us and love Jesus' Church. President, help us, you who are our friend. We don't know any more what to do. We are in despair.... We are in yours and in God's hands.

The elders of the Church in Livorno offer us their help and love, but they can't baptize us without our parents' permission.... We can't bear it that we can't get these things until we are 21 years old. What should we do?

We would be very happy if you would answer our letter. We need your words. If you could answer, we would be very grateful. We've heard that very probably you'll come to Munich with the Mormon Tabernacle Choir. We would like to meet you and listen to the wonderful choir. We are praying a lot so that the Lord will make our dream come true to go to Munich.... Please, pray for us, too. Help us and we promise that we'll be strong and will always smile.... We give our testimony and our love for the Church and you....

Mariella and Rita Colombo

In reply, President Lee wrote the following on July 20, 1973:

I believe I have never read a more inspiring letter from one of our young people which has impressed me more than the beautiful letter you wrote to me recently about your feelings and desires with regard to one day becoming baptized members of The Church of Jesus Christ of Latter-day Saints. As I looked at your beautiful pictures and noted not only the outward beauty you two have, I also seemed to discern the beauty of your characters. I was grateful that the Lord, in an unusual way, had led you to come in contact with our missionaries who have given you a taste of the glories of membership in His Church and the blessings that can be yours if you will follow the teachings of our Lord and Savior, Jesus Christ.

Your letter, indicating that your parents, at the present time, have not been willing to hear the missionaries or give consent for your baptism, reminded me of an experience I had some years ago concerning a young girl just over legal age who had been baptized despite the opposition of her mother who was very bitter when she joined the Church. She later went to the temple and there she received a wonderful promise from the president of the temple that if she would live worthy and keep herself morally clean that the influence of the gift of the Holy Ghost, which was pronounced upon her when she was baptized, would affect those with whom she came in contact who would oppose her in her righteous desires and she would be able to overcome their opposition.

Some weeks following her visit to the temple, she wrote a letter back to the president of the temple in which she described her reunion with her mother, who began as she had done previously—cursing, profaning, and threatening to disown her daughter; but this time the daughter did not quarrel with her mother. She put her arms around her mother's shoulders and led her over to the couch and sat down beside her. She leaned her cheek to her mother's and told her the joy that she, the daughter, had experienced while being active in the Church, and particularly the wonderful experience in going to the holy temple. Then she bore her testimony to her mother, and to her delight her mother burst into tears and begged her forgiveness. This girl then closed her letter saying, "We are now preparing Mother to be baptized a member of the Church."

This will happen to you if you let your parents, in due

time, see the gospel through your lives, as that mother realized the truth through her daughter. You could be the means of bringing your parents to one day realize the great joy that you are experiencing.

While we talked about your experience, my wife, Joan, and I remembered a visit we had to the Italy South and North Missions last September. There we met one of our splendid missionaries by the name of Filippo Magistro who is living in Rome.

He is a year older than the average missionary and is well acquainted with the missionary program. It occurred to us that if this splendid young man might come in contact with you and perhaps your father and mother, he might be the means of answering your prayers. It seemed as though this ... was the inspiration ... through His Son, our Lord and Master, to help you. Through this medium with your faith and prayers answered, you may begin to realize the fondest desires of your hearts.

Keep yourselves clean and worthy. In the wickednesses around you, as you have described it, there will be many temptations. Some of these may profess to be religious, but be on guard and hold yourselves in such a way that the Lord can work, through you, the miraculous spiritual influence that can be yours to all with whom you come in contact, and one day the promises of the Lord will be yours and you can look forward to a great and successful life as wives and mothers and leaders of the young people in your own home and among those with whom you labor. Please know that you have my love and my blessing and trusting that I may hear from you again as you progress in our Heavenly Father's work.

Affectionately yours,
Harold B. Lee

Notes
[1] Translation received from the President's Office

23

Name Withheld

"A Testimony of Tithing"—H.B.L.

Little did this faithful couple realize that when challenged to live fully the law of tithing, they would lose all they had, but through greater faith, find the power to rebuild their lives.

At one time I called Elder Lee on the phone seeking counsel with regard to the payment of tithing inasmuch as my wife and I had just received a sizable sum of money in the form of stock rather than in cash. I didn't tell him this but I had asked my bishop, my father and one of the General Authorities, and all had made the same judgment: Pay your tithing when you receive the money in actual cash.

Feeling extremely restless, I called Elder Lee because even though all my advisors had agreed, it didn't seem correct to me. And the brief moment he gave me convinced me completely that the counsel I had previously received was not correct.

Elder Lee counseled us to borrow the necessary funds to pay our tithing, then said something like this: "As surely as you do this, the Lord will pour out inspiration and revelation upon you in your home and in your assignment in the Church, and you will know whether this has been the right thing to do."

Then a letter came to us in the mission field from my partners informing me that a large sum of money had been deposited into my account in the bank at home because of the favorable earnings during 1967 in one of our businesses. The interesting thing about it was that it was almost enough to complete the payment of that debt we had been carrying since Elder Lee gave us that counsel.

Far more important than the possible freedom from debt, though, is how greatly the Lord has favored us with His Spirit in our home life. We have tasted of the love that living the gospel principles brings into a family. And we have tasted of the love that service in the missionary cause has brought into our lives. The promised inspiration and revelation have indeed come to pass.

We returned from our mission to resume work in our profession and enjoyed success as the business prospered. Calls to serve in other positions in the Church came to each of us. Again we learned how wise President Lee's counsel had been. We heeded, and we enjoyed, those gifts of "inspiration and revelation" he had promised to us if we faithfully paid our tithing.

Years elapsed, and there were reverses in the business. Our personal assets, our share in the business, and our other holdings eroded away considerably almost overnight. We faced the traumatic decision of selling our large family home that was so oriented to our large family of children and grandchildren, that was among neighbors whom we had grown to love and cherish. Other assets were liquidated to meet our personal obligations, but we made it without having to resort to bankruptcy. When the dust had settled, so to speak, we had nothing.

Keeping our heads erect and looking for the "light in the tunnel" was the most difficult of all the trials we experienced. Stress and strain were at the highest levels they had ever been in our business affairs. Had it not been for a marvelous companion and a wonderful family and loyal friends, all these adjustments in our life could have been disastrous.

We learned that assignments to serve in the Church helped us to keep matters in better perspective. Bitterness and animosity had to be discarded from our lives. We learned that we must be as forgiving of others as we expected others to be of us.

We struggled trying to locate new employment or some kind of opportunity that would provide the means to live. How far-reaching was President Lee's advice? Did the promise of "inspiration and revelation in all you do" apply to the temporal as well as the spiritual? The logical conclusion was that it did.

Stern lessons in humility were learned as our standard of living dropped from the level it had been to what it became. Day by day we plodded ahead looking for opportunities. Our kind bishop came to our home one night, in the midst of this, and offered assistance if needed. Fortunately we had a supply of basic foods that we could draw from, but few can appreciate what one goes through when retirement plans have been obliterated, along with assets accumulated over years of diligent work.

In the midst of all this turmoil the account of Nephi and his brothers kept recurring in our minds as "they presented their gold, silver, precious things before Laban." Laban not only lusted after their wealth, he even threatened their lives. Almost humorously, it seems, Nephi said, "We were obliged to leave behind our property—it fell into the hands of Laban." Like Nephi's family, we too lost all our wealth.

It was as if a light had been turned on in our minds as we realized that we were having that very experience. The cord that bound them to Jerusalem and their past had to be severed for them to move on with the work the Lord would have them accomplish. New strength would have to be drawn upon if they were to make it through the ordeal: And come it did—but not without testing their faith. Nephi's injunction, "Let us go up again, and let us be faithful in keeping the commandments of the Lord," could have been directed to us.

The light began to brighten as we recalled young Nephi with his marvelous faith: "Being led by the Spirit, not knowing beforehand the things which [he] should do." Yes, our retirement benefits were gone. Whether or not we could measure up to a new challenge in our older years was to be determined by us. The test of our mettle was on the line. Was President Lee's counsel applicable in this new set of circumstances?

Day by day we began to see our prayers answered as inspiration flowed in simple, wonderful ways, but not without our struggling to do all we could first. Who, we wondered, would ever loan us the funds necessary to start a new business as we were nearing retirement age? A close friend who was aware of our situation asked if he might help in some way. At the same time an opportunity developed. We asked our friend if he would be willing to loan us a considerable sum of money at a reasonable rate of interest. He indicated that he would. As he wrote the check for a sizable amount, he said, "Now if the time comes that you are unable to pay this money back, remember that this is only money, and friendships are far more important than money. My wife and I will pray for you to be successful and we will do all we can to support you in this new business."

Two other friends responded in a similar manner. These two men and their wives knew how risky this proposed venture was, but they had trust in our ability and knew that we would be willing to sacrifice whatever was necessary to repay the debt.

Next came the task of finding a place to live. A dear friend in the real estate business knew of a condominium for sale that might be rented with an option to buy within a couple of years. We jumped at the chance and began renting. It required some sprucing up, which was done with the help of our family, to bring it up to standard, but it proved to be a very habitable place to live.

As the new business was about to open, once again our family of sons and daughters and their companions, as well as our brothers and sisters, pitched in and helped us in our preparations for our opening. They saved us hundreds of dollars by giving of their time and effort. No one will ever know how many tears we shed as our hearts filled with gratitude for these wonderful loved ones and what they did for us.

One of the great blessings through all of this monetary loss was the strengthening of family ties. We who had been able to give in years past because of our abundance found ourselves on the receiving end, a difficult position for us to accept. Our hearts were filled with love far beyond anything we had ever known.

The new business had a difficult time the first year because it had not been established long enough, and we had no assets to pledge to provide funds for additional cash needs. Had those with whom we did business known how heavily leveraged we were in those first months, they never would have extended credit to us. But our friends who had loaned us the money knew of our experience and trusted our judgment. That expression of confidence was a vital part of the healing necessary to keep moving forward after suffering the loss of our interest in the previous business.

We worked feverishly to succeed. This necessitated our working without personal compensation for several months to pay the monthly interest due each of the friends who had loaned us the funds. Gradually, and consistently, we chipped away at our credit debt in our business by paying our bills promptly. Conditions now were looking brighter and our business continued to grow in a solid manner.

After a few more months we were able to raise a small down payment on the condominium, and the owners were willing to take a contract with us on the balance for five years. As we were unable to qualify for a commercial loan due to our smaller incomes, this was a heaven-sent opportunity. Later, the owners were willing to extend us another five years on the payout of the loan because we had made our payments promptly to them each month.

As we exercised discipline in reducing our standard of living from what it had been, my wife taught music to over forty students in the home in order to supplement our income. Without her wonderful support and constant encouragement, we might never have made it. She never complained; she just worked as busily as I did. At one point, however, she was hospitalized for a serious illness. Her blood supply was so weak that several blood transfusions were necessary to keep the oxygen flowing throughout her system. Her life hung in the balance for several days.

It was during this period of time that I learned how important it was for me, her husband, to diligently seek the Lord's help for her, not only through priesthood administrations but in prayers that had an earnestness to them I had never had occasion to exert before in her behalf. It was at this time that the Lord taught me how important she was to me and to our family. I learned that she was one of the very choice daughters of the Lord. That came by the manifestation of the Spirit as I pled for her life. How marvelous all of this was to comprehend. Without this adversity, how much we might have missed. She made it and lived!

As each day commences, we thank the Lord that we are blessed with health and strength to work. Our business has enjoyed success, though we have had to work long hours to avoid hiring any more employees than absolutely necessary to keep current on all our day-to-day obligations.

We have discovered that our lives have been like climbing a ladder—a step at a time—and with each step, a new lesson in obedience and gratitude to the Lord, to inspired servants of God, whom if we obey, blessings follow.

How often we recall the sage advice of President Lee, one whom we honor as "a prophet, seer, and revelator." Little did we realize that the advice given 27 years ago would not only affect our lives for a few months, but would serve as counsel that was relevant our entire lives. As we raise our voices in singing the hymn "We Thank Thee, O God, for a Prophet," a broadened meaning has come to us as we look back with a deep sense of appreciation for President Lee, who counseled us in our younger years with great wisdom. We will ever be grateful that he was "at the crossroads to show us the way." Now we realize that we also must show the way to our own family as they come to similar crossroads in their own lives. We must never be quitters in the sojourn through life, but must press forward with faith.

Dr. Gordon Jensen

Beverly Jean Jensen Woodard

My Father's Miracle

"Dr. Gordon Jensen was healed from leukemia, or at least arrested—Dr. Wintrobe pronounced him healed from this dreaded malady."—H.B.L.

My father, Dr. Gordon M. Jensen, of Logan, Utah, was diagnosed with chronic myelogenous leukemia in May 1956. I was three years old at the time. On May 28, he asked Elder Harold B. Lee to administer to him and to give him a blessing from God that he would recover from that fatal illness.

He also underwent the chemotherapy treatments that were available at that time. In August of that year he was advised by his doctor that he was in remission and that he could discontinue the medication that he was on. His blood work appeared to now be normal and he had returned to work. He wrote the following letter to Elder Lee on August 12, 1956:

> I feel that I must take a moment of your busy time to bring you up-to-date on myself. Since that blue Monday, May 28, when you administered to me I have made a most remarkable recovery. Two days ago Dr. Wintrobe told me I was now normal again and could stop the medicine. I will be followed at monthly intervals. I now feel better than I have for several months.
>
> I am trying to follow your counsel and advice to the very

letter—in fact, my family and all my relatives are. I have been working a full schedule for over a month and seem to be able to do it without difficulty. No one in my profession could have made me believe this in May, but when you left my room I felt as if I had been born again and I believed with all my heart that I would through some miracle be restored to health. I only hope that I can serve the Lord and help others sufficiently to be worth the saving.

I always enjoy receiving a letter from a patient telling me he is doing well. For this reason I thought perhaps you might like to know that your "patient" is doing very well and is eternally and deeply grateful. Also, I am much better prepared mentally and spiritually to meet reverses in the future. Please accept my humble and sincere thanks and appreciation. May the Lord continue to inspire you and watch over you and keep you in your wonderful work.

For nearly three years from the time of his diagnosis my father was able to continue working. In January of 1959 he became gravely ill and passed away on February 3, 1959. By that time I was six years old.

Three years does not normally seem to be a very long time, especially to an adult, but to a child of three, three years is, literally, double your lifetime! Between the ages of three and six a child goes through much of the learning processes that will serve him for his lifetime. Those are the years when you learn how to read and write, you start to make decisions for yourself and begin a formal schooling program. You also start to take notice of relationships between people and start to form relationships of your own. The events that you later remember about your life generally begin around this time.

I don't know what my life would have been like if my father had died shortly after his diagnosis, as was quite common back then. In those days medicine wasn't nearly as progressive, or as successful in the treatment of disease, as it is now. There weren't treatments like bone marrow transplants or the modern chemotherapy drugs and radiation therapy that can ward off or even cure these diseases. I do know, however, that my life was completely changed because of those three years!

My whole family and I were truly blessed by having those three extra years with my father. I was able to really get to know him, not to just have my memories be what other people told me about him. I was able to sit on his lap and learn to read, to have both my mother and father take me to my first day of school, to begin to see and understand the truly loving and sharing marriage between my parents.

I also was able to spend a significant amount of time with him in his office at the Budge Clinic in Logan. That was where I found out that I also had a love for medicine and decided at an early age that I would like to become a part of the medical world. In what capacity that would be, I didn't know until I was about eighteen years old, but the seeds were planted way back then. My final decision about the field I would be in was largely based on my father's illness. I am now a medical technologist in a blood bank. I work with and prepare special blood components for leukemia patients and others that have had bone marrow transplants.

My older sister and I were both able to learn about illness and death and coping in the face of adversity. We were able to see how faith in God and strength in the family can guide one through the really hard times. We were able also to learn that love and laughter within the family can be the glue that holds it together. We learned that even though conditions aren't always how we would like them to be, we have to believe that God's plan for us is Divine and that His will must be honored.

This entire experience, however, wasn't just about me. My father was the one to whom all this happened. He was the one who had to deal with the fear and the pain and the unknown of each day that passed. He had to make the decisions that he knew would affect his family for the rest of their lives. I believe he knew his remission was temporary and that he needed to do what he could for the comfort and security of his family before he died. He was allowed the time to make the necessary plans and arrangements for my mother to be able to support and care for my sister and me. He was able to make certain we would be well taken care of and that my mother would not have to go back to work.

He was diagnosed with leukemia only three months after moving to Logan and setting up his medical practice there. What a frightening experience that must have been for him—he was in a new town, with a young family, and a deadly disease. His remission allowed him to continue in his practice for almost three years. This length of time was a blessing not only for our family, but for the people in Logan as well. He had gone to Logan because they were in great need of a surgeon at the hospital there. He was able to spend the time necessary to help his patients and to find a qualified replacement for himself.

He made the decision early on that he needed to make the best of his situation. He worked closely with his doctor, the foremost authority on leukemia and blood disease at the time, Dr. Max M. Wintrobe. He spent hours documenting and tape recording every aspect of his illness, before and after his remission, and then again when his disease recurred. He wanted to have the most accurate documentation that was possible so that other patients might be helped by his experiences. Dr. Wintrobe acknowledged my father in several of his medical textbooks and papers. I believe some of their work together has led to the more advanced treatments and procedures that are now being done for these kinds of patients. I know that was my father's hope.

It is difficult, at best, for someone to decide exactly what elements are required in an event to classify it as a "miracle." I know that I am not qualified to make that decision. Even so, I truly believe that there was a "miracle" in my family. I believe that through faith and prayer God allowed my father three years, two of which were disease free, to begin to raise, educate, and instill values of worth in his children; to make arrangements to provide for his family after his death; to care for his patients in Logan until a qualified replacement could be found; and also to help, both directly and indirectly, people in the future who would also be afflicted with the same disease that took the life of this noble young father and husband.

25

John E. Wiscombe

The Reality of Satan

> *"John Wiscombe (uncle of ex-Superintendent of SLC schools Arthur Wiscombe) tells of Satan's taunting when he was afflicted with boils while serving as an elder in San Francisco in 1921."*—H.B.L.

As a missionary in San Francisco in the year 1920 or early 1921, I spent my entire mission at 1649 Hayes Street. The chapel and rectory there, which had been purchased from some sectarian church, served as the conference headquarters. Our sleeping quarters were upstairs at the rear of the building which faces north on said street, making the bedrooms on the south.

I had been afflicted with boils, they being confined chiefly to the back of my neck and a few also on my hand and wrist. I suffered the torture of this affliction, in all, for two months or more, near the close of which period I was almost despondent because of it. During the same period, or most of it, our conference president, Wilford W. Richards, was also afflicted with this same trouble. We did almost everything that people would suggest to try to rid ourselves of the disease, but it seemed we could not effect a cure. Most of the time the siege was so severe that I could not perform my regular missionary work, although it would usually clear up sufficiently for me to care for my many duties on Sunday.

One day I was alone in the house and in bed in the west bedroom. The head of my bed was against the west wall of the room near the north wall. At the southeast corner of the room was a window in which were two sashes; each was approximately 30 inches square and opened on hinges to either side. The bottom of the window was approximately two and one-half feet from the floor.

During my illness I had tried to take advantage of the time in studying the scriptures and how to present my message to the people, but on this day, I felt so miserable I decided to go to bed. I had learned that a long siege of affliction will shatter the nerves of the strongest of people. (How I admire the faith, the strength and the fortitude of Job!)

It was probably the deflection of light that caused me to turn my head toward the window as I was lying on my back, for I had heard no sound. As I did so, I observed a figure entering the window in a hurdling position, face forward with the left leg already through and the foot apparently on the floor. Amazed, I gazed at him as he entered the room, as if stepping in from mid-air. He was clad in some garment comparable to tights or a bathing suit, with the arms and legs almost wholly bare excepting the upper part of the thigh. He was as fine a specimen of physical man as I have ever beheld, being approximately six feet tall with an almost perfect muscular body to match his height. His course was straight from the window to the middle of my bed, where he stopped, folded his arms, and looked at me.

I was very much startled, at least in my feelings, but was too weak to become very excited physically. (I am naturally quite calm, even under pressure.) But even though it all seemed so real, I still could not trust my vision so I proceeded, as I lay there, to pinch myself with the thumb and forefinger of both hands, commencing with my ears, my cheeks, my neck and on down my body to my feet, to assure myself that I was awake and that what was passing before my eyes was a reality.

My physical weakness must have been apparent to him as evidenced by his only remark: "You're a fine emissary of the

Master—to allow a thing like that to get you down. Where is the power you claim through him?" This was said with a caustic sneer as the most devilish expression I have ever seen crossed his face. It was so penetrating that for the moment I fairly quaked— in fact, I despaired of my very life. But it was only for the moment, as I raised myself on my left elbow to a partial sitting position, and in the most majestic experience of my life, point- ing the index finger of my outstretched right arm, I commanded: "By the authority of the Holy Melchizedek Priesthood, and in the name of Jesus Christ, GET OUT OF HERE!"

Instantly the hellishness of his taunting expression left him, and apparently the fear that had been mine completely over- whelmed him. His countenance fell and like a skulking pup he backed out of the room and window without turning, keeping his gaze upon me as he had done from the time of his first appearance, and vanished as stealthily as he came.

The ordeal was too much for my physical strength and I fell back upon my pillow exhausted, yet awake and conscious. I was conscious sometime later (I don't know how long) when Brother Richards came to my room. When he saw me he turned very pale and anxiously inquired how I was. I told him I supposed I was all right but weak, and then I related my experience. His comment was, "Great Heavens, man, what else must you pass through?"

Later, when the other boys came in he called them together and related briefly what had happened. They unitedly adminis- tered to me, and I commenced an immediate recovery and in a few days was able to happily go about my work as usual. My recovery was very much expedited by the kind and affectionate ministrations of Brother Richards, whom I shall always love.

I know not why this experience came to me unless it was to impress me with the fact of the reality of the adversary—his power to take upon himself a bodily form in which to carry on his diabolical mission among men, and his power to prey upon the weaknesses of people. Perhaps it was given to demonstrate to me the marvelous powers of the Priesthood even when exercised under dire physical weakness. Or perhaps it was for both reasons. I only know that I have wondered greatly as to the full meaning of it. Perhaps it was given to fortify, to strengthen, and to enlighten me for future events in life. Since that time I have witnessed a similar expression on the faces of men in a few instances when I have known them to be possessed of a devilish spirit.

Although my suffering from this affliction was grievous and I regretted very much the loss of time and effort in my work, this period gave me the greatest opportunity of my life to study and concentrate on spiritual matters. As a reward, to compensate, I suppose, for these unpleasant experiences, I was given an insight into what seemed to be the true social and economic order which the Lord would have men live; where the effort of each and all is expended in the interest of the fullest development of the individual, regardless of his capacity, and of society in general. There was no usury; no profit-taking from other men's labors. The development of the person was the sole aim.

The vision of this so impressed me that since then I have tried to practice the philosophy of such a society, dedicating my life, in the main, to public service both in church and the community. It is not always easy to abide by such a philosophy. There are many difficulties and hardships suffered which are unknown to any but God. Public service means a sacrifice of time, energy, and often money, all of which means the giving up possessions considered of social and economic worth by most people. But to me it is a wonderful ideal to work toward and I trust the Lord will give me strength to sometime gain that goal which was so beautifully portrayed to me in that vision.

* * *

Jack's nephew, Arthur C. Wiscombe, wrote later:

Jack ("Johnny") Wiscombe was the eighth child of eleven born to William Fleet and Sarah Newland Wiscombe, in Springville, Utah, on December 3, 1888. He grew up in that small central Utah community and graduated in due time from Springville High School. He married Margaret Miller, and they eventually moved to the Uintah Basin, Roosevelt, Utah, to make their home. In their marriage four sons and one daughter were born and nurtured by them.

Jack made his living as a skilled painter and an interior decorator, and was subsequently employed for many years by the Utah Power and Light Company as an accountant. He gave much of himself to community service. One notable example is his selfless devotion in serving for some twenty-seven years as a member of the Duchesne County School Board.

His gospel doctrine class in the Roosevelt Ward gave him some modest intellectual fame. He was believed by many to have been the most reflective teacher of religion that many "had ever known."

In 1919 he was called on a mission and served in California. He left his wife and family at home in humble circumstances and completed an honorable mission. It was during that assignment that he experienced an open face-to-face encounter with Lucifer, the "son of the morning," as described here. He related it many times to family and friends over the years, and formally recorded the event and presented it to Apostle Harold B. Lee at his request.

After a full and rich life, Jack Wiscombe died in Roosevelt, Utah, on April 26, 1947.

26

Lenore Romney

Ten More Years to See

Twice Elder Lee administered to Sister Romney, who relates the blessings received and promises fulfilled.

When my eyes started to fail in 1964, I asked Elder Harold B. Lee for a blessing, which he graciously gave me. Soon thereafter my husband, George, and I went to see Dr. Charles Campell, who was head of the department of ophthalmology at the College of Physicians and Surgeons at Columbia University in New York.

Dr. Campbell noted cystic formations generally diagnosed as macular degeneration, which is irreversible. "But," he said, "the formation is not typical and inasmuch as there is no treatment for this, I'm going to give an alternative diagnosis. This follows one of three courses: (1) it responds to certain types of treatment, (2) it can be arrested from further degenerative processes, and (3) it follows a progressively degenerate course rapidly in spite of any treatment.

None of the other opthalmologists I had seen gave me an alternative diagnosis. And most interesting was that Dr. Campbell used Elder Lee's words in explaining to me that I must search out the treatment that was most effective and study and test each method.

Dr. Campbell also stated that this alternate diagnosis was based on a condition caused by spasms produced by allergic reactions causing constrictions to the eyes. Elder Lee had referred to this vascular restriction in the blessing he had given me, and had prayed that my circulation should improve in *all parts of my body.*

Elder Lee's blessing promised me (contingent upon my faith, of course) "complete peace of mind" with the spirit ascending over the physical. According to Dr. Campbell, one of the essential ingredients in treating this condition is for the patient to have complete peace of mind. Dr. Campbell said further that emotional stress and worry over the condition further constricted the blood vessels.

How I soared with the promise of these holy words! I had been blessed with the most essential component for my improvement *peace of mind* as well as an improved circulation. Knowing that I would need more than my own wisdom, I felt secure in the knowledge that special help from above would be brought to instruct me. I had already been granted celestial help in determining the proper treatment. How I marveled at the beauty and magnificence of Elder Lee's words and their import.

Indelible upon my heart, these words would light my faith and my life. My eyes, the windows of the soul, as they are described, were to light my way as long as the Lord had work for me to do. I would have all my faculties until my mission had been fulfilled. How magnificent to have been told in a blessing that I did have a mission yet to fulfill.

* * *

My eyesight did not deteriorate for another 10 years. I was able to have driving privileges until 1977. Then my sight gradually became dim.

Now, 30 years after the blessing, at age 85, I still have all my faculties although my eyesight is now quite poor. Throughout the years, I have had peace of mind, knowing I would be blessed through my life; and indeed I have been! Great opportunities and experiences have been mine with my wonderful late husband. Until recently, I was still racing through airports holding onto George's dear hand, and traveling a great deal of the time.

I am reminded now of another remarkable blessing Brother Lee gave to me. I was in severe shock from a blood transfusion in which the new blood did not match completely. I was in such severe shock that I was almost shaking off the bed. My heart too was racing wildly. My doctor said I would have many such episodes, but Elder Lee blessed me that I would be healed immediately. My shaking stopped at once and never occurred again. This was indeed a miracle. I know Elder Lee had the gift of healing.

I do not in any manner boast of these blessings. I am humbled by the Lord's blessings and feel unworthy indeed to be so blessed. I have authorized these accounts, hoping they will reveal God's goodness and His giving of special gifts to His servants.

* * *

President Lee's personal journal entry of Saturday, October 30, 1954, contains his impressions of this second episode. He was in Detroit to attend the Detroit Stake Conference shortly after Lenore's husband, George W. Romney, the stake president, was appointed president and general manager of American Motors. President Lee wrote:

> Shortly after we arrived [at our scheduled welfare meeting], a message was brought to President Romney that his wife had suffered a relapse from a hospital accident when calcium being injected into her blood had gone throughout her arm and shoulder, causing a serious infection and inducing a severe shock. The president invited me to accompany him to administer to her at home. When we arrived her hands were icy cold and numb, and her heart was beating wildly. She was very much afraid.

> We administered to her and under our hands she testified that her heart adjusted itself and returned to normal. A great peace came over her and all anxiety left her. She was overwhelmed with gratitude and felt assured of a wonderful blessing. I insisted that President Romney remain with her while I returned to conduct the leadership meeting with the stake and ward leaders.

Alice Smith[1]

Testimony Valued over Health

Elder Lee told her in a blessing that she would fall to her knees and thank God for her affliction as an arthritic cripple, and she did.

It was hearing Elder Harold B. Lee speak, shortly after I was baptized in 1943, that helped me to bear the cross of being crippled from arthritis from the time I was 22 years old. I haven't walked for over 25 years. I had gone to my first district conference in June 1943, and Elder Lee was the speaker from Salt Lake. He spoke to the congregation for about 10 minutes, then stopped. "I had a speech prepared for tonight," he said, "but for some reason I can't go on with it, so I will tell you something else." He told us about a young girl whom he knew who came to him for a temple marriage recommend. She was going to marry a young man who was very badly crippled. This young couple felt that life was short and they would have all eternity together when he would be well and strong.

After the meeting Elder Lee gave me a blessing that banished the bitterness from my heart. It stilled my doubts and fears and helped me understand my affliction.

Even so, I have often wondered why I haven't been healed by the priesthood. The Lord has seen fit to heal a kidney that was eaten away on one side by an ulcer. Because of the power of the priesthood, the surgeon didn't have to remove the kidney. Another time I was operated on for what the doctors thought was cancer of the liver. They found the liver badly damaged, but there was absolutely no trace of cancer. It was healed. The doctors didn't know what to make of it.

And yet, I am an invalid. In spite of my crippling arthritis, I have spent six years as M.I.A. president and have taught several years in the M.I.A. as well as four years in the Relief Society and more recently I have been busy doing genealogy work. I have gained a great deal of knowledge from these callings and I am very grateful for them.

With the assistance of my husband, Lowell, and that of the officers and teachers, we kept the young girls busy with numerous projects. There were baked food sales nearly every week all summer to help with the chapel building fund. Later, yard sales were held at the local park to pay for transportation and lunch for Swarm Days, which were then held in Richland, Washington. Most of the Beehive classes had more nonmember students than LDS members.

At another time in my life, Elder Lee later gave me second priesthood blessing for my health. I had been feeling very weak and it seemed as though my very life was being crushed out of me. He told me that Satan and his angels were trying to destroy me so that I could not fulfill my mission. He promised me from that day forth they would not have any power over me and that I would live to bring many persons into the Church. He told me not to complain and God would take me by my hand and show me what he wanted done, and when I had finished that work he would take me home.

Elder Lee said the time would come when I would fall to my knees and thank God for the sufferings and tribulation he had let me bear. At the time I didn't see how that would ever be true. Nevertheless, if I could have my health back in exchange for the knowledge I have received through this affliction, I would not trade them. The gospel has been the greatest blessing I have ever received.

Notes

1Sister Smith was a sweet, courageous woman. The word "handicap" was not in her vocabulary. She died August 27, 1978, having been a member of the Church for 35 years.

28

June J. Cavalli

From Despair to Joyous Accomplishment

Elder Harold B. Lee blessed this 14-year-old boy suffering from an unknown illness. At age 18 he was cured and lived a useful, inspiring 19 additional years.

At the age of fourteen, my son Don was suffering from an unknown illness. In April we sought the medical advice of Dr. Max M. Wintrobe at the Salt Lake General Hospital and the University of Utah medical staff. He diagnosed the disease as disseminated lupus erythematous, a disease that is incurable but that can be controlled. He then sent us back to Ogden, for he felt our doctors there had done a good job.

Our son, however, grew persistently worse. In May he was used as a case study at the medical convention held annually in Ogden. The decision of all the doctors and specialists there was that he had a form of cancer and perhaps also lupus. With this verdict he was again placed in Dr. Wintrobe's care.

During this trying period, the words of a blessing my son had received at the hands of Elder Harold B. Lee were ever present. We were told that he would be healed "according to the faith of his parents," so my husband and I fasted and prayed and asked our friends and relatives and friends to do likewise. We placed Don's name on the prayer rolls in the temples. We did our very best to keep on with our church positions and in every way tried to keep the commandments of the Lord to the best of our ability, so we would be found worthy of having our prayers answered. Don's faith was an inspiration to us all. Elder Lee also prayed that his illness would become known and a treatment found.

The trials of the summer of 1958 are still vivid in my mind as the doctors continued to fight for Don's life with steroids and chloroquinn. Throughout this time, Elder Lee's words never left me. They were a guiding light to me during this time of hopelessness as Don lost so much ground that he could hardly walk without falling. The steroid gave him a myriad of side effects, which, added to his illness, were a source of despair to us. At last, the steroid finally got Don's lupus under control; by January 1959, Don was back in school. From that point on, he improved steadily.

The final diagnosis of Don's condition was that he did not have cancer, just lupus, which was ultimately controlled with minimum doses of steriods and chloroquinn.

Don's health improved so much that he was able to wrestle on his school team and play basketball with the ward, in addition to skiing and bowling. He was also able to hold down a part-time job while maintaining excellent grades. To look at him, one would never know how ill he had been.

As his nineteenth birthday approached, Don was apprehensive. He so strongly desired to serve a mission, but he was afraid he wouldn't be accepted because of his medical record. In June 1962, Don turned 19 and was called to the Swiss-German Mission. There he labored in Germany, Switzerland, and Italy for two and one-half years, speaking German and Italian. He completed his mission holding positions of leadership and returned home the summer of 1965.

While on his mission Don had another bout with lupus and an accident during which he fell down an elevator shaft. Concerning these adversities his mission president, John M. Russon, wrote to us:

Once again the Adversary has tried to deal a mortal blow to your son, but again the Lord intervened and kept him from disaster. Once again we recognize the hand of the Lord in watching over your son in his time of greatest need and we are grateful that his life has been spared again. He surely must have a great mission to fulfill.

* * *

In 1966 Don was married to Carolyn Fowers, with whom he had three sons. After receiving his bachelors and masters degrees, he became the director of District Two Council on Criminal Justice Administration, where he served for eight years. In addition to his several Church callings, he also taught police science at Weber State College at night. He also had an illustrious career with the Utah Jaycees, which culminated in an appointment as one of the ten national vice-presidents of the U.S. Jaycees in 1976-77. The U.S. Jaycees present annually a memorial award to honor the service of Don Cavalli.

Don lived to the age of 34, when he died from cardiac arrest caused by sepsis. When I read of President Lee's death, I was able to accept our son's passing without any further reservations. I thank our Father in Heaven for answering the prayer offered on his behalf so many years ago which gave us over 19 additional years of his life.

Don lived an extraordinary life, a life full of commitment to the principles in which he believed. Though frequently ill, he never complained and never seemed to rest long enough to recover. His faith in God sustained him throughout his life and his service to humanity continued until the day he died.

29

Harold B. Lee

Called to Duty by a Heavenly Voice

President Lee recalls the story of a bishop who heard a voice telling him that a family in his Star Valley ward was without food, and he responded in time to answer the prayers of a faithful mother.

During World War II, the body of the Church was not invited to attend General Conference because of the limitations and the dangers of travel at that time. The Brethren called a special testimony meeting just for stake presidents on the fifth floor of the Salt Lake temple. After the sacrament had been administered, the stake presidents bore their testimonies. The testimony of President Ballantyne of the Southern Arizona Stake particularly touched Elder Harold B. Lee, who later related President Ballantyne's story at the Seminar for Regional Representatives of the Twelve, on Thursday, September 28, 1967.

I was raised up in Star Valley, Wyoming [President Ballantyne had said]. It was a hard, difficult climate, the soil not too good, and we struggled. Father had a large family, and sometimes after we had our harvest there was not very much left after expenses were paid. So Father would have to go away and hire out to some of the big ranchers for maybe a dollar a day, a little more than to take care of himself, and a very little to send home to mother and the children. And things began to get pretty skimpy for us.

We had our family prayers around the table, and it was one such night that Father was gone that we gathered, and Mother poured out of a pitcher into a glass for each one, milk divided among the children, but none for herself. And I, sensing the fact that the milk in the pitcher was all that we had, pushed mine over to Mother and said, "Here, Mother, you drink mine."

"No, Mother is not hungry tonight," she said. (Mothers are never hungry in cases like this.) That worried me.

We drank our milk and we went to bed, and I could not sleep. I was the oldest in the family. I got up and tiptoed down the stairs, and there was Mother out in the middle of the floor kneeling in prayer. She did not hear me as I came down in my bare feet. I dropped to my knees and I heard her say, "Heavenly Father, there is no food in our house today. Please, Father, touch the heart of somebody so the children will not be hungry in the morning." When she finished her prayer, she looked around and saw that I had heard and she said to me, somewhat embarrassed, "Now you run along to bed, son. Everything will be all right."

Well, I went to bed assured by my mother's faith. The next morning I was awakened by the sounds of pots and pans in the kitchen, and the smell of cooking food. I went down to the kitchen and said, "Mother, I thought you said there was not any food." All she said to me was, "Well, my boy, didn't you think the Lord would answer my prayer?" I got no further explanation than that.

Years passed and I went away to college. I was married and I came back now to see the old folks. Old Bishop Gardner was now reaching up to a ripe old age, but he still had a keen memory and as I visited with him he said:

> "My son, let me tell you of an experience that I had
> with your family. I had finished my chores, and we had
> had supper and I was sitting and reading the paper. My

shoes were off and I was sitting by the fireplace. I heard a voice that said, 'Sister Ballantyne doesn't have any food in her house.' I thought it was my wife. I called out, 'What did you say, Mother?'

She came in wiping her hands on a towel and asked, 'Did you call me, Father?'

'No, I didn't say anything, but somebody did.'

'What did they say?' she asked.

'It said that Sister Ballantyne didn't have any food in her house.'

'Well then,' she said, 'you better put on your shoes and your coat and go over and take some food to Sister Ballantyne. Somebody is telling you to do your duty as a bishop.'"

Under cover of darkness that night Bishop Gardner took flour, meat, potatoes, and all the necessities, because he was acting in the office to which he had been called and under the impulse of the power of the Almighty God.

After relating this experience, Elder Lee closed with these words, "Now we too are in His service. We have the right to that kind of spiritual direction, if we live for it. God grant that we may ... not fail of the high appointment for which we have been called in our Father's Kingdom."

30

Betty Jo C. Reiser

A Child of Promise

After four years of longing for another baby, this mother received a priesthood blessing from Elder Lee and conceived almost immediately thereafter. The promised baby was named Harold, one of more than a dozen so named under similar circumstances.

Both my husband and I were raised in large families and always we had hoped and planned for a large family of our own. Within four years of our marriage we had two handsome young sons whom we loved and enjoyed. However, as they grew older our prayers for more children remained unanswered. After nearly four years, and after numerous tests and consultations with specialists, we were unable still to have more children.

At that time I was serving as the ward Relief Society president. We had numerous welfare projects, which included sewing men's work shirts and women's slips, and we were also involved in monthly welfare and building fund dinners. These were in addition to our regular Relief Society duties of planning and conducting meetings, visiting the sick and compassionate service. We were having an ambitious bazaar for which we had planned and prepared for a year. I also was responsible for the Relief Society sacrament meeting program.

Since our ward consisted mostly of young couples, we spent many hours visiting, helping, and serving our young mothers with their new babies in addition to everything else. Ward members and friends knew of my longing for more children. The longing was made more evident as I had almost daily contact with sweet, newly arrived little babies.

One day while visiting a new mother, the father, who was aware of my enjoyment as I held the baby, said, "I can tell by your actions you'd like to have another baby. Maybe that would happen if you stayed home and stopped running around using up your energy doing Relief Society work and helping others."

At his words, I burst into tears. The new mother was chagrined at her husband's suggestion, and she scolded him. She knew of our deep desire to have more children. The young father was embarrassed and he apologized. In turn, I explained, through my tears, that I didn't feel I could expect my Father in Heaven to answer my prayers for more children if I didn't continue to serve him to the best of my ability.

I often confided my disappointment at not having more children to my dear friend and visiting teaching companion, Helen Goates, whose father, Harold B. Lee, was then a member of the Quorum of the Twelve Apostles. (Helen's husband, L. Brent Goates, was our bishop.) One day Helen asked if I would like a special blessing from her father to help accomplish our desire for more children. Although I had had other priesthood blessings, I was nevertheless delighted at her suggestion.

I made an appointment to go to Elder Lee's office, where he gave me a wonderful blessing promising that we would have other children. In less than a month thereafter I knew we were to have another baby. We named our third son Harold Lee Reiser. He was an unusually happy baby, as if he sensed the joy he brought to our family. His nickname to us and in the extended family was "Happy Hal." Many family members and friends asked if he ever cried. (We finally took a photograph of him as he was crying so we could show he really did cry on rare occasions.)

Whenever Elder Lee met Harold he would remind him, "You are a child of promise." Then he would give him a dollar to put into his missionary fund.

When Elder Lee visited our stake as a General Authority, he bore testimony saying that, "Miracles have occurred in the homes of this stake. Through the power of the priesthood, women who were barren have borne children and the sick have been healed." I knew he was speaking of me, along with others.

After serving a mission to Brazil South Mission, Harold attended the University of Utah, graduating with a master's degree in Business Administration. He later graduated from the University of Utah College of Law.

His name has been a constant reminder of the power of a priesthood blessing through an anointed servant of the Lord. Along with Harold's beautiful wife, Janet, and their three adorable children, Rachel, Adam Harold and Alexander, much joy has been brought into our lives through our son's miraculous birth.

31

*"Whom I love,
I also chasten..."*

D&C 95:1

D.L.

"Opening the 'Book of Life' to a Confused Girl"—H.B.L.

Correspondence with Elder Lee saves a young girl from the disaster of involvement with a married man. Obeying, she found her happiness in worthiness for her temple marriage.

Dear Elder Lee:

I write to close a chapter in my Book of Life that you opened for me before I start a glorious new one, and close a chapter in your volumes of correspondence that I opened.

About five years ago you received a letter in your office from a very confused girl. You must have wondered at that time how anyone could be so foolish—she surely must have known the answer [to her questions].

She did. She asked what was right and I can't imagine why she hesitated to act, but she did. That girl wrote that she was in love with a married man and felt she had a right to help him....

You wrote just what she expected, told her she had no right to even think of him and that she should leave [the area].

She did leave, right away, just as far away as possible so she wouldn't be tempted to return to her home too soon. That opened the most wonderful period in in her life. She again became, as she had been before leaving home, active in the Church. She was called on a stake mission and then on a full-time mission, where she met a young man with whom she became more acquainted, when she returned home from the mission.

She is now working as a secretary at Brigham Young University, and is planning to marry the missionary she met on her mission. It is the happiest occasion of her life. I never knew life could be so wonderful and I am so grateful I left before it was too late five years ago. I am so thankful I can take a clean body to the temple to be married to a clean fellow.

I'm not proud of that period five years ago, but I am determined to let it be a lesson to me and live the rest of life in righteousness so I may be worthy to be a companion to my future husband.

I wish every girl could realize how important it is to be able to take a chaste body to the temple to be married. It's a priceless gift....

I am supremely happy now. Who knows how miserable I might have been? I am so glad that the sentence doesn't read, "How miserable I am because I made the wrong choice."

P.S.—I know I have a wonderfully beautiful life ahead if I will make it such. I hope and pray that I can.

*Initials only used at author's request.

R. Viola Davidson

A Healing Handshake

A U.S. sailor with a most painful swollen, infected arm shook hands with Elder Lee after a servicemen's conference in Tokyo, and was immediately healed. He was baptized a few days later.

My husband, Floyd Thomas Davidson, was a U. S. Navy career serviceman, very handsome and blessed with natural leadership abilities. He was not a member of the Church when we were married, but the year 1954 brought a wonderful change to our lives.

Floyd was aboard the U.S.S. Hornet on a round-the-world tour of duty. On board that ship an outstanding Latter-day Saint servicemen's group was organized. He mingled with these men and wanted to be like them. Soon his conversion neared, and he planned to be baptized when they arrived in Japan.

The group was excited to learn that Elder Harold B. Lee of the Council of the Twelve was touring the Orient and was to preside at a servicemen's conference in Tokyo. Floyd, too, wanted desperately to attend this conference, but he had developed a most painful, swollen, infected arm. The ship's physician also was a member of the Latter-day Saint group and gave him permission to go ashore for the conference since he would be there to attend him if necessary.

Floyd was uncomfortable throughout the meeting, but after the conference he lined up to meet and shake hands with Elder Lee. Floyd told Elder Lee that his aircraft carrier would be in

Manila at the time Elder Lee would be visiting the Philippines and that he hoped he would see him then and be able to tell him that he had been baptized a member of the Church.

While on the train en route back to the ship in Yokosuka, Floyd suddenly realized that whereas the pain in his arm had been almost unbearable all during the meeting, the severe pain was now completely gone and his arm had been healed.

A few days later, I received a telegram from Yokosuka, dated August 27, 1954: "Baptized this morning. Now your Latter-day Saint husband. Love, Floyd."

Floyd was privileged to see and visit with Elder and Sister Lee in Manila. In October Elder Lee spoke to a general conference audience in the Salt Lake Tabernacle and quoted the following from a letter Floyd had written him:

> Something happened to me after I left that conference in Tokyo. My arm was swollen and was painful all through the meeting, but after I had shaken hands with you, I got on the train going back to the boat. Suddenly the pain ceased, my arm was healed, and now I am going back to that lovely wife who has been praying that I would straighten my life. I smoked, and I drank, and I did a lot of things to cause her sorrow, and I am going back to that sweetheart of mine, and I am going to spend the rest of my life trying to prove myself worthy of her love.[1]

For 30 years my husband was a living testimonial of how Elder Lee changed his life. Floyd became a wonderful husband and father and an outstanding member of the Church, serving in many positions, including that of bishop and high councilor.

Floyd's health began to fail in 1979, and he passed away on November 3, 1984. I am so grateful for his true and lasting conversion and his worthiness that led to our marriage for "time and for all eternity."

Notes

[1]Elder Harold B. Lee, in *Conference Report,* October 1954, pp.128-29.

33

Clifton I. Johnson

Three Miracles

Three children desired baptism under adverse conditions, and their wish was granted. One of them was miraculously healed at the same time. Years later, a man was given one month to live, but a blessing by President Lee extended his life for five-and-a-half more years.

I have had the joy of witnessing miracles from President Lee during my younger years and also as a mature man.

In 1948 I was a full-time missionary living in Portland, Maine, and serving as a conference leader of the Southern Maine District of the Church. Elder Harold B. Lee presided at a special district conference that was held there. Also attending was our mission president, Elder S. Dilworth Young, a member of the First Council of Seventy. Elder Lee invited several of the missionaries to speak, and they bore beautiful testimonies, after which President Young then spoke followed by the apostle.

After his sermon on the subject of sacrifice, Elder Lee asked everyone in the audience needing a special blessing to come forward at the end of the service. A young lad who was to be baptized on the following day was one of those who responded to his invitation. The fifteen-year-old boy, Lee Hamblin, had had an accident while working in the forest with his father, a lumberjack foreman, and had badly cut his hand with an axe. Blood poisoning had set in and his condition was serious. Elder Lee gave him a beautiful blessing.

The next day, Saturday, we all met at Longfellow Square, which is part of the Dearing Oaks Park in Portland, for a baptismal service. The weather was very dark and dreary, and it had been raining for several days. Two faithful members, Brother and Sister Rossborough, had gone to pick up the six Hamblin children and their mother who were to be baptized. The father, Mr. Dana Hamblin, had given his written consent for his children to be baptized although he had been very bitter toward the Church for some time. He had finally given his permission to have his six children baptized; however, because it was raining so hard, he now refused.

"The children cannot be baptized unless it stops raining and unless the sun shines," he said.

The children were heartbroken, but Brother Rossborough said, "Your father didn't tell you not to attend the baptismal service. And bring along your clothes, just in case."

As we neared the resort lake of Watchic, and turned down the main road to the lake, President Young commented that it had stopped raining although it looked like it would start up again at any time. When we stopped on the shores of the lake the children gathered about President Lee, crying and sharing their story. He said to them, "Don't you cry. Put on your clothes. You will be baptized."

Despite his words, the weather was so dark and dismal that none of us had much hope. After the prayer, several people were baptized. Suddenly the sun broke through the dark overcast like a spotlight beam on the waters. Elder Lee said, "Come now, let's not keep the Lord waiting. Let's get these Hamblin children baptized."

The first of the Hamblin children was young Lee Hamblin, who had been administered to by Elder Lee. After his baptism Lee felt under his arm and hollered to his mother, "Hey, Mom, the lump's gone!" And so it had. It was not only a day of miracles for his arm to be healed, but it was also a day of miracles that the six Hamblin children could be baptized because the elements were brought under control.

At the conclusion of the services Elder Harold B. Lee offered the closing prayer, thanking our Heavenly Father for his tender mercy and guidance to us that day.

I later had the blessing of baptizing in Utah the father of those beautiful children. In time Brother Hamblin himself became an excellent missionary, converting and baptizing many people.

* * *

Many years later, I was serving as a bishop in Bountiful, Utah, and was visiting a ward member at the hospital. George Alder, the member, was being attended by Dr. Jewel Trowbridge, a very competent and well-respected physician. Concerned about Brother Alder's health, I followed Dr. Trowbridge into the hall and asked him the severity of Brother Alder's illness.

"He has a very severe case of multiple myeloma," was the doctor's reply. He explained that George had a cancer of the bone and gave him, at the most, one month to live.

Elder Lee was called upon to give George a blessing, and he came promptly to the hospital. Elder Lee blessed George and promised him that his life would not be shortened one whit because of this illness. He told him that he would live out his life according to his time allotted by our Heavenly Father. It was a beautiful blessing and lasted over 15 minutes.

It was my privilege to visit George on numerous occasions over the next few weeks and to observe that Brother Alder never complained about his illness. Two months from the time of George's hospitalization and blessing, my wife and I and our six children left for our mission to Burningham, England. We were thrilled to see Brother George Alder personally come to the airport to see us off.

Upon our return from the mission in July 1971, the new bishop of the ward asked me to be George's family home teacher. We shared many wonderful spiritual moments. One evening we went to his home and enjoyed a wonderful family home evening with his family, as we all joined together in wishing him a happy birthday, and seeing him enjoy life with the zest and vigor that he had. While he was not entirely able to get out and move outside of his home, his mind was still clear and keen. We felt this was wonderful, four years after the doctors had said there was no hope.

As promised in President Lee's blessing, George's life was indeed extended and his death was not from the multiple myeloma. George passed away on November 11, 1974, at the age of 68 years from kidney trouble, some five and one-half years after he was blessed by Elder Lee.

Les Goates

Blessed in the Language of Adam

Harold B. Lee and Lesley Goates shared grandchildren. On March 27, 1949, after Elder Lee had named his third grandchild, he wrote in his diary: "I asked Les Goates to relate his testimony concerning the blessing he had received in tongues when he was blessed as a 3 lb. premature baby."

Quite a long time ago in a little country town not so very far from Salt Lake City, a mother sat weeping and praying over what was supposed to be an infant son. I say "supposed to be" because this little one, although almost seven weeks old, weighed only three pounds. In addition to its infinitesimal size, the infant also suffered from a serious physical deformity.

In those days there were no incubators for premature babies, so this one was kept in a small basket with medicated cotton for its bed. Folks came from miles around to see this tiny freak of nature—especially doctors, who shook their heads and went away. Of course, everyone knew, the child would not live very long.

But the mother never ceased to fast and pray that her little one might be spared. She never relinquished for a moment the absolute assurance that she would yet rear her babe. Her faith was astounding. Then, one day in March of 1894, her husband's father, William Goates, came down from his big house on the corner through his beautiful garden to the little shack by the rail-road track to offer any help that he might render to the distraught mother and her child.

The rugged old pioneer took one look at the infant in the basket, then said to the mother, "Louie, I want you to give up this baby and let it go. We all know that only your faith and your prayers are keeping it alive. The time has come now for us to look out after you. Why, you haven't been able to walk only a few steps at a time since the little thing was born. Now we must look out before we lose you, too.

"Besides, suppose that by your faith and your prayers, this babe is permitted to live. Chances are, it will be a lifetime burden to you and your family all the days of its life, for the doctors say it can never amount to anything. I think it best that we give it up, and let its spirit go back where it came from."

Louisa Munns Goates said nothing as one more tear dropped upon the old, home-made rag carpet. Her father-in-law picked up his hat and strolled back through the garden, through his front gate and up the street to the town meeting house where the monthly fast and testimony meeting was about to convene. In those days fast meetings were held on Thursday afternoons.

Presently George Hyrum Goates, the father of the infant came into the house. George too looked at the baby, heaved a long sigh that seemed to convey the attitude of discouragement and despair, and said to his wife, "I don't think I can do any good here, Mother. I'll go down to the Old Field and do some more plowing. The ground is getting dry and every day at plowing helps the crops that much."

He hitched his team to the wagon and drove over the railroad track and down the road to his little farm. The rattle of the wheels as they bounced over the rails had scarcely died away when the mother said to her sister-in-law, "Sarah, we are going over to the fast meeting and get the baby a name and a blessing."

"But how can we go to the meeting?" Sarah protested. "We have no horse or buggy, and you have scarcely walked since the baby came."

"We'll manage somehow," the mother remonstrated. "I'll take

this small rocking chair, drag it along for a few steps, then sit down and rest. You can carry the baby. He is very light."

So, in that strange way, these two women made their arduous way to the Lehi meeting house on a Thursday afternoon carrying a wee babe and a rocking chair.

When they arrived the babies already were being blessed. The wee infant was given a name and a blessing under the hands of its maternal grandfather, James Munn. This man was a patriarchal-looking gentleman who was bent over and scarred from the mobbings he had suffered in the old country because he was "running away with the Mormons."

After this ordinance had been attended to, the time was given to testimony bearing and among others there arose to speak a woman of rare spirituality, a Sister Mary Elizabeth Woffinden. She spoke of the many gifts and blessings she had received through the gospel, and expressed her gratitude that she had been "privileged to come from old England to the land of Zion."

She then began to speak in a strange language, a smooth, melodic tongue that sounded like sweet music. As she spoke she occasionally made a gesture toward this mother with the small baby, so that the audience understood that she was speaking about them.

When she had finished, James Kirkham, the stake patriarch, arose to interpret the testimony. "This sister has spoken in the language of Adam," he said, "and she has conveyed a message and a promise to this mother who has fasted and prayed so long for her little one." It was on account of the exceedingly great faith of this mother, he said, that her prayers had ascended to the high heaven and her child, who had been appointed to come into the world only long enough to receive an earthly body, would now be privileged to live, to grow to manhood and rear a family in Zion. He would perform a work of which this mother would be exceedingly well pleased, the patriarch concluded.

How much easier and shorter were the steps back home to the little old shack by the railroad track! When they arrived there, assisted by kind neighbors and friends, Sarah undid the baby's wraps to make it comfortable and as she did so she exclaimed excitedly, "Louie, Louie, come here quick! The baby! He's perfectly all right!"

The mother ran quickly to her baby and found that all signs of physical deformity had disappeared; the child, in very truth, was perfectly normal.

That woman of great faith was my mother, and I was that wee one who was blessed in the language of Adam.

* * *

From Dr. William T. Black's *Mormon Athletes*[1]:

This blessed infant grew up to become one of the best sportswriters of the century. A comment made by other famous sportswriters, Damon Runyan and Grandland Rice, on one of their visits to Utah showed his status: "You know, that fellow, Les Goates, is one of the greatest writers in the United States. He deserves the best."

His achievements as a journalist are countless and his writings some of the most memorable in newspaper print. It has been estimated that over his 44-year career he wrote at least 10,000 columns (six days a week) and over 500 verses, all appearing in *The Deseret News.*

Les Goates was the initiator of all-state prep basketball teams in Utah and in the United States in 1919. For 29 years his acclaimed "Les' Go by Les Goates" column appeared on the sports page, making it the longest continuous daily sports column in any Western newspaper. He helped organize the Utah-Idaho Baseball League and the Pioneer Baseball League, and was the official scorer for the Salt Lake Bees in the old Pacific Coast League. He glamorized the "Golden Era of Sports," making champions such as Jack Dempsey, Bobby Jones, Bill Tilden, and Babe Ruth glitter for his readers as if set with diamonds.

A coach once said, "Les Goates has produced more all-Americans than Ike Armstrong [the University of Utah football coach]." At Les Goate's retirement banquet, many of Utah's finest athletes who were present said: "If it hadn't been for Les Goates

I don't think the athletic world would have known I was around. He helped me to become what I was in the world of sports."

Les Goates hired them to write sports when they were in danger of dropping out of college before the days of athletic scholarships, and in emergencies, loaned them money during Depression years.

Even with his many activities in the athletic world, Les never lost sight of other values of life. He gave much service in music and to his Church. He was a Sunday School music director and superintendent and the ward choir director. He served as bishop of the East Mill Creek Ward for ten years. He was also a stake high councilor and a Salt Lake Temple ordinance worker.

For 50 years he was a singer and director of choirs, including 20 years as director of the Symphony Singers (women's chorus), and seven years as director of the Associated Women's Choruses of Utah, which he helped organize.

Elder Mark E. Petersen said of Les Goates that "during the latter part of his career he made a most important contribution to the public relations of the Church for his work as a special writer for the Public Communications Department. Masterful writings from his pen appeared in newspapers far and wide in the U.S.A. and other countries as he plainly taught high gospel principles in articles which were published by these newspapers both as editorials and as special features."

Les Goates lived to father a family of five children and was finally taken in death in 1975 at the age of 81.

Thus, it was indeed a work of which not only his blessed, faithful mother also could be proud, but untold thousands of readers were blessed by his writings, which were always refreshing, edifying, and even inspiring, and ever sprinkled with both good humor and good sense.

Notes

[1]From William T. Black, M.D. *Mormon Athletes, Book Two* (SLC: Deseret Book, 1982), p. 256-262.

Brenda Wood

The Greatest Miracle of My Life[1]

Even the death of President Harold B. Lee dispelled the darkness and confusion of this lost convert and pointed the direction to safety, peace, and home.

I grew up in the country some 70 miles north of Toronto, in a fairly well-developed rural area. My parents used to tell me stories of people getting lost in the "bush." Although there was a fair amount of bushland around us, it would have been pretty hard to get lost in it.

To a small child, though, it had seemed huge. I was always fascinated, in a terrified sort of way, by my parents' stories. People were often found a mile or less from safety, and yet they would have wandered for hours, sometimes days, in circles. Some might eventually find their own way out; others were found and rescued. And still others were found too late.

I used to wonder what I would do if I got lost. I had heard that if you could locate the North Star in the sky at night, you could use it as a guide. So I used to study the myriad of stars in the sky trying to find the Little Dipper and the Big Dipper, and the North Star. When my oldest brother got a compass, he tried to teach me how it worked.

But I could never seem to decide which star was the North Star, no matter how many times it was pointed out. I just couldn't understand the compass. I wondered why would I want to walk north if I were lost, particularly if home was west or east? But then, I could never seem to keep the directions sorted out, either.

My confusion and lack of direction were representative of my life. Having grown up in a world that lacked stability and security, I decided very early that the world was a dangerous, terrifying place, where no one could be trusted. I knew there was a God, but I was afraid of him. I thought He was a God of judgment, and I was of no consequence, for if He loved me, why didn't he protect me as a child? I decided that I was so bad that He didn't want anything to do with me.

By the time the missionaries brought the gospel to my door, I had exhausted every resource that I knew, and it seemed that none could decide if north was even north, never mind anything else. I knew that I was totally, hopelessly lost, that I was wandering in circles, and had been for years. The feminist movement told me I was wasting my life staying at home raising my children. Another group said I should have only one child, and that if I had any more I was contributing to the overpopulation of the earth. Other groups claimed that earlier generations had messed up the world, so we should go off to live in communes, grow and smoke pot, and get hooked on love and peace.

The missionaries gave me a Book of Mormon, and as I read it I wanted more than anything to believe that it was true. I needed something stable to build upon. But I was afraid that I would be deceived as I had been so many times before. I didn't know how to trust myself. And I certainly didn't know if I could trust these young men who were sharing messages that I had never dreamed of before.

Finally, in desperation, I tried one more time. I called out to the God who I was no longer sure was even there. It was then that I received an answer and a testimony of the gospel was branded upon my soul. The missionaries had always said, "If you have a testimony of the Book of Mormon, then you have a testimony of Joseph Smith as a prophet. Likewise, if you have a testimony of the Prophet Joseph Smith, you have a testimony of the Book of Mormon."

Well perhaps, I should have told the missionaries about my

poor sense of direction. I didn't have a testimony of the Prophet Joseph Smith; I just didn't think much about him. And the present prophet at that time, President Harold B. Lee? Well, he seemed like a nice man, what little I knew of him.

I was baptized on December 16, 1972. A year later, on December 26, 1973, President Harold B. Lee died. As the news of his sudden death flashed across my television screen the following day, I looked into the face of this man and I was overwhelmed by a sudden feeling of loss and sorrow. And the Spirit bore witness to my soul that this man was a prophet of God.

Whereas the logic of the missionaries didn't convince me, this surely did. If President Lee was a living prophet of God, then Joseph Smith also was a prophet of God, and so were all those in between.

It still seems so strange that it would be the death of this gentle man that would burn the testimony of living prophets into my heart, and give me the greatest gift of all—a compass, my very own North Star, that could guide me for the rest of my life, pointing always towards home.

As I have pondered the great blessings of having a living prophet, I have struggled to find the words to express something that overwhelms me in its immensity. The knowledge that there is a living prophet on the earth, as spokesman for the Lord, is like a cornerstone that holds together the whole foundation of the gospel for me (see D&C 1:38 and D&C 21:4-6).

I have learned that I can trust. I can feel safe and secure. The words from scriptures have been distilled into my mind and heart. The world may still feel terrifying and dangerous, but I need never be lost, wandering hopelessly in circles. It is like the North Star and the compass exercises long ago, though I have found that it is not enough to just know. It is necessary to use the compass, and use it consistently.

As I have followed the directions of the living prophets, as I have sought diligently for a testimony of their words, I have received, line upon line, all the gifts necessary to heal the confusion, the fear, and the pain in my life. The fear has been replaced by faith in a living God who testifies to his servants, the prophets (see Amos 3:7).

My confusion has been replaced by a testimony of eternal truths. I know that "I am a child of God"; that I am of infinite worth; that God lives and Jesus is the Christ; and that the gospel in its fullness has been restored, including the blessing of a living prophet. And the pain has been healed by love, the love of my Heavenly Father, and of my Savior, through an understanding of the miraculous power of the Atonement.

* * *

A few years ago I was interviewed by a reporter from the *Toronto Star* regarding the illness of President Benson and the highly advertised excommunications from the Church. My comments, as well as those of other Church leaders, were reported, and the tone of the article was very critical. However, the testimony burned into my very soul and bones so many years ago was like a fortress. I was so grateful for that, because of the verbal battering I received from the reporter and the resulting backlash from the article that resulted in the opposition of even those who are considered strong members of the Church here.

I sometimes wonder what my life would be like if I had never received that testimony of President Lee as a prophet of God. I think I might not have had the strength to withstand the fires that I have been through in the ensuing years.

I know that my Heavenly Father is always mindful of me and that He brought the gospel into my life so that I could work out my salvation and return to Him. I didn't realize in those early days and years that that meant healing the wounds in my mind, body, and soul that I had received during many years of childhood abuse. I came to the gospel heartsick and broken, and was miraculously healed, although it was not easy.

I struggled then, and still do to some degree, with my childhood history, as do all survivors, because one of the greatest deficits with which we are left is the inability to trust—not only others, particularly men—but ourselves. Probably of the two, the most debilitating is the lack of trust for ourselves. We constantly second-guess our decisions and our intuition.

For me, the testimony of prophets begun so simply that day has meant that I can rely always on at least one person on this earth. Testimony is synonymous with trust. Should doubt cloud my reasoning, should fear cause me to flounder, I need only refer to the words of the prophets to find my way back to solid ground.

The living prophets have been the light in the darkness for me. Their goodness taught me that not all men are the same. As I felt of their love, I was able to build a relationship with my Savior and with my Father in Heaven. The prophets, as living men, were links for me to a Savior and a Heavenly Father who were also men.

My Heavenly Father understood my needs, and He provided a way for those needs to be met. I have no words to express the debt of gratitude that I feel for all that He has done for me. And so I follow the example of my Savior, and the prophets and apostles, and I serve them in gratitude.

In addition to my over three years of service as the stake Relief Society President, I have also have served throughout the wards and stakes of Southern Ontario in a volunteer capacity with survivors of abuse.

It has taken a number of years for me to recognize the miracles that have occurred in my life, for I thought, like many people, that miracles were something great and marvelous, and the miracles in my life have been quiet. Nevertheless they have been both great and marvelous. Through the gospel I have found a healing available nowhere else. Through the gospel I too can testify as did the Prophet Isaiah:

> "They that wait upon the Lord shall renew their strength; they shall mount up with wings as eagles; they shall run, and not be weary; and they shall walk, and not faint." (Isaiah 40:31)

Notes

[1]Excerpts from a talk by Brenda M. Wood at the Toronto Stake Conference, 13 March 1994.

Diana Bird Holt

He Has Kept a Light Burning in My Life

In the matter of a moment, my life changed from activity and fun to pain and bed confinement.

In April of 1968 I was in a very serious accident which has caused no end of trouble. What was once a very busy and active life in the Pep Club at Highland High School in Salt Lake City—playing tennis, water and snow skiing, swimming, and dating—came to a screeching halt when the car I was in slid on snow and rammed into a mountain throwing me through the window. My head and neck took the force of the blow and since that time I have been in chronic pain and spent over two years of days and nights in the hospital, endured five major surgeries on my spine, been through two pain clinics and spent hundreds of thousands of hours horizontally, coping with endless pain and facing the constant threat of paralysis. In the matter of a moment, my life changed from activity and fun to pain and bed confinement.

After spending weeks in and out of the hospital, I went through a period of time where I was sleeping for extended lengths of time—from Monday night until Wednesday afternoon, or from Saturday afternoon until Tuesday—until the clouds would finally leave my senses and life would slowly come back into focus.

After one of these episodes I was with my daddy, who was sitting on my bed. He had given me some pain medication and was talking quietly to me. His voice was so comforting and encouraging and yet I was afraid to go to sleep because I thought that I might not awaken until the next day or perhaps ever! I poured my heart out to Daddy and explained my fears.

"You need a special blessing," he said. "Is it all right if we set that up for you?"

A phone call was made to reach Elder Harold B. Lee. Only a brief explanation was given: "Diana is very ill and needs a blessing. Would that be possible in the near future?" Nothing was said about the accident, the great pain or hospitalizations, just that I was very ill and needed a special blessing. Elder Lee said he would begin fasting that moment and my parents were to bring me to his office the next day.

As Mother and Daddy gently prepared me and dressed me for the outing that day, I remember thinking that it was crazy to go to all this work and more pain to go "out" for a blessing, no matter who was giving it. I opened my eyes only once but I do remember sunshine and warmth, as Daddy and Mother and my Aunt Leah took me to Elder Lee's office.

Daddy, who had hugged and loved my pains away countless times, propped me up in a large wingback chair. Elder Lee asked him if he would like to join with him in this blessing. Daddy told him that he held the Aaronic Priesthood and Elder Lee asked him to be seated. This was done in such a sweet, gentle manner that it precluded any possibility of hurt or embarrassment.

Elder Lee came around in front of me and took my hands in his. "Diana," he said, "the Lord has a very important message for you today and I feel privileged to be His mouthpiece."

He then went around behind me and gently placed his hands upon my head. I was somewhat embarrassed because not all of my hair had grown back since it had been shaved off for my surgery after the accident.

Elder Lee's first words in the blessing took me completely by surprise and shocked a silence into the room that was deafening!

"Diana Bird, at the time of the accident the Lord saw fit to place His finger down upon your life and save it, for you have not yet completed what you've been sent to earth to do."

I looked up and saw shock on the faces of Mother, Daddy and Aunt Leah. It was silent for a few moments, almost as if Elder Lee was allowing us time to absorb the impact of that mighty sentence. At exactly that moment, the three of us realized that I should have been killed in the accident. We also understood that Elder Lee had received divine inspiration during the blessing because he had no previous knowledge of the accident or the damages.

He then continued with several encouraging promises, which have helped to raise me above the tides when the undertow of pain seemed to be drowning my desire to live and endure another day. He told me that I knew before I came here the pain and suffering I would be asked to endure in this life, and yet, when the day came for my arrival here on earth, I rejoiced. I had a guardian angel, he told me, whom I knew and who would, on many occasions, intercede for me when I had a close encounter with death. (This has happened on three occasions already. I have no doubt about this promise.)

Elder Lee blessed me with patience and a kind heart, and told me that my pain would enhance my ability to give strength to others in their time of need. During the two years that I was a Hospice Family Advocate Counselor I used my knowledge and experience to comfort others; and it brought many hours of calm reassurance to my troubled heart. Working in the emergency room allowed me to share my knowledge in a positive way and gain greater perspective myself. It is hard to have a personal pity party when others are in more serious condition. Those hours of service brought a deeper relief than any shot or pill ever could have. It was an opportunity to serve instead of being served all the time.

Elder Lee said I would be blessed with a husband who would be a strong priesthood holder, who would help me during my struggles, and that I would live to raise a good family. Those blessings have been fulfilled in wonderful ways.

He also told me that I would be a mighty instrument in the

Lord's hands and that I would have many opportunities to speak to groups on a large scale, and further, that my experiences would become powerful teaching tools. I have indeed been blessed with many opportunities to teach. I have never turned down an offer with two exceptions when I was hospitalized for surgery. I have spoken to youth groups, Relief Societies, leadership meetings, stake camp firesides and others. I spoke at a Tri-Stake Youth Conference in Dallas, Texas, and to the LDSSA at the University of Arizona. Two months after I spoke they awarded me with the Elect Lady of the Year Award, and it made the pains, experiences, and trials seem worthwhile and important. I have also taught many groups how to care for chronically or terminally ill people. Instead of feeling nonproductive and unnecessary, I have felt like a tool in Heavenly Father's hands.

I am clinging to one more promise that has not yet come to pass. President Lee told me that "there will come a day when you won't be able to remember the last time you were in pain." In the last nineteen years since the accident, I have spent a total of two years of days and nights in the hospital and have survived five major surgeries with the promise of more to come.

These promises and blessings are the primary source of my strength from which I have drawn comfort thousands of times. Nothing could persuade me not to believe that these words and the other words of the blessing were directed from the Lord. Elder Lee never knew what an impact that his blessing had on my life. He died before I could tell him how much the blessing encouraged me to hang on, even hour by hour.

How can I express how much that blessing has meant to me over the years? I am not bitter; I am no longer angry or afraid. I do not ask for miracles, just for strength and peace of mind during the roughest times. My Heavenly Father blessed me that autumn day to meet a man of great faith who had an overwhelming desire to comfort a frightened little girl. The blessing Elder Lee gave me has kept a light burning within me for oh, such a long, long time.

I share this experience with the hope that it will bring faith, hope, and confidence to others to believe in their Priesthood blessings. Each day, when my eyes become accustomed to the light, I have a sense of wonder and awe at the miracle of life. My being able to *celebrate* it for these extended years is due in large measure to this special blessing I received from Elder Harold B. Lee. My gratitude knows no bounds.

* * *

Diana's husband, R. Douglas Holt, submitted the following not long after Diana's death in 1995.

Diane wrote the foregoing account of her life in 1988 at the request of L. Brent Goates, to whom she is related by marriage. The following years were full of additional joy and challenge. Her family's understanding of God's purposes in pain expanded.

Mostly from home and bed, Diana supported me while I served as a bishop, in the stake presidency, and in numerous callings. Rarely was she able to attend a ward temple day or a stake conference. Her back and neck continued to deteriorate. In 1989 she sought a priesthood blessing for advice on how to support me in my callings, but obtained the unwelcome divine counsel to undergo additional surgeries to her neck and back, as God had a calling that would require greater health from her.

In the middle of these surgeries, a telephone call came from a member of the Quorum of the Twelve Apostles requesting an interview. The two of us went to see the Apostle on a day immediately prior to her third surgery that year. Her faith in Elder Lee's blessing was astounding, as she recounted to the Apostle the promises that had been made and the additional feelings she had about missionary work and her commitment to building the Kingdom.

In spite of her hospitalization five times that year, and four more surgeries, the Lord accepted Diana's willingness to serve as a mission "mother," and she and I were called to preside over the

Portugal Lisbon South Mission, in December 1989. She had known by revelation that this call had been coming, and she felt that the Lord would strengthen her for the task ahead. She left for Portugal in June 1990 with great faith and without pain medication, traction devices, or other pain management tools.

The schedule was rigorous, the roads rough, and the weather extremely cold. In spite of it all, Diana persisted in trying to fulfill her assignment. She received additional priesthood blessings from other brethren who came through Portugal, including President Gordon B. Hinckley and Elder Spencer J. Condie. Her missionaries constantly prayed and fasted for her.

Throughout the year of her mission in Portugal, she taught her missionaries to love each other as well as the people. She lived an example of Christlike service, striving to make the missionaries comfortable in the mission home, in spite of her increasing pain. Her talks bore the stamp of faith, as she witnessed in zone conferences of the power of God's many miracles in her life. Her special gifts of compassion and understanding were applied to heal the hearts and lives of numerous missionaries.

Diana's mission to Portugal lasted 13 months. She came home for medical consultation and learned that she should not return. Soon the whole family followed.

Four years later, after consecutive weeks and months of increasing head pain and suffering the effects of heavier medication, Diana was released from her mission in life by her Father in Heaven. The day promised by Elder Lee had finally come. Having honorably completed the mission her life had been preserved to fulfill, she is now without pain.

Diana died on October 2, 1995, in Tucson, Arizona. Over 2,000 persons attended the funeral service in her honor in Tucson, and a week later nearly 1,000 persons crowded a ward building in Salt Lake City where a memorial service was conducted.

Helen Lee Goates

The Miracle of the Silent Doorbell

How far does the miraculous influence of President Lee reach? This story tells how, after his death, his home and the irreplaceable family treasures within were spared when the roof threatened to collapse due to heavy snow.

"On no!" I thought to myself that Saturday afternoon. "What else could go wrong?" Our doorbells had been malfunctioning all morning, ringing intermittently when no one was at either the front or back door. When I reported this to my husband, he made a quick investigation. To our surprise, he found they didn't ring at all. We had invited our ward temple group—about 35 guests—to gather at our home the following Tuesday evening and I was annoyed at our faulty doorbell. We decided to contact an electrician the following Monday morning.

This was in February of 1993, a winter of record snowfall in Salt Lake City. Storm after storm piled snow to unprecedented heights, causing extensive damage to the roofs of many dwellings. My husband and I had been away in Israel for two weeks during the heaviest of the storms, labeled "the storm of the century," which broke all records for snowfall in a 24-hour period. Schools had been closed, and most activity came to a halt as residents began the arduous task of "digging out."

When Brent and I returned home after our trip, we had been amazed at the huge snow banks surrounding our house.

Nevertheless, we were happy to return to our home, made more dear to us because it had housed my beloved parents before us. My father, Harold B. Lee, the eleventh president of the Church, had purchased the home in 1961. My mother had been so thrilled with it that she always called it her "dream home." She had lived there, contented and happy, not quite a year before she died.

My father had subsequently married again, and he and his new wife continued to enjoy the home together until his death in 1973. My stepmother remained there until her death in 1981. We felt there was a special spirit these loved ones had left behind, one which my husband and I hoped to perpetuate in this home when it became ours.

We had only been home a few days when we began to hear creaking sounds. One morning I heard a definite cracking noise coming from the living room area at the front of the house. Upon investigation, we were appalled to find there were cracks in the walls and evidence of unmistakable structural damage in each corner. We immediately called a young man to come the next day to shovel the snow off the roof to relieve the weight. The creaking stopped, but the damage remained. We contacted the insurance adjuster, who, already "snowed under" with similar demands, was unable to come.

So, on that Saturday before our ward temple group was to gather in our home, my impatience with yet another problem, even a minor one like a faulty doorbell, was understandable.

The electrician came to repair the doorbell late Monday afternoon. "The problem must be in the transformer," he said. He looked in the basement, but failing to find the transformer, he went up into the attic to look for it. Moments later, he called down with unmistakable alarm in his voice, "Mr. Goates, do you have any idea what damage there is up here?! It looks like a war zone!"

My husband followed him up and was dismayed by the broken beams everywhere and the severely bent struts. The ridge of the roof had been split open by over three inches.

Fearing that the roof might collapse at any time, the electrician was reluctant to stay there longer; but before he left, he strongly urged us to call for an expert opinion.

In light of this new development, we made arrangements for our supper party to be transferred to another home in the ward. When Arnold Fluckiger, our home teacher and a busy architect, heard of our plight, he appeared at our door the next morning, bringing with him a business associate who was a prominent structural engineer. We had not called either of them; they came out of concern. They concluded that we were indeed in jeopardy of our roof collapsing over our heads. They recommended immediate removal of the new snow on the roof and a covering of heavy plastic over the entire surface.

"But if you hear one more creak," the engineer warned us as he left, "get out immediately!"

As we were unable to locate anyone who could help us relieve the oppressive weight on the roof, our home teacher, fully sensing the danger, went home, changed his clothes, put on his heavy boots, and returned to do the job himself. Over our repeated protests, he climbed up on the roof and began the task that lasted until dark and all the next day. It was truly an act of Christian love.

The emergency "band-aid" treatment was accomplished and the immediate danger was over. More storms came, but this time the snow slid off the roof.

At last, we were able to get the attention of the harried insurance adjuster. Three competent contractors began preparing bids for our home repairs. Arnold, our home teacher, drew up complete drawings of the structure, and the engineer made his recommendations. Our home and its irreplaceable contents would soon be safe and secure again.

A few days later, I was alone in the house and was startled to hear the doorbell RING. I went to the door, expecting that no one would be there. To my surprise, I found a salesman at the door. After he left, I pushed the bell again to test it. It rang loud and clear, as did the doorbell at our back door, just as they had done so faithfully for the eleven years we had occupied the home. What had caused its mysterious malfunction? And why, now, without any repair, had it begun suddenly to operate again?

Doorbells are intended to allow visitors to obtain the attention of the occupants within. Had a visitor, unseen and unheard, sought to gain our attention to warn us?

As we pondered this question, comfort and reassurance came that someone, somewhere, was mindful of the dangers to the physical structure of the home that had such a heritage of family happiness. We received the assurance that, through the brief malfunction of a most reliable doorbell and perhaps, even with the help of loved ones beyond the veil, God had protected our home.

"God also bearing them witness, both with signs and wonders, and with divers miracles." (Hebrews 2:4)

Elder Joseph Anderson

J. Robert Anderson

The Call of Elder Anderson as a General Authority

President Harold B. Lee set apart Elder Joseph Anderson as an Assistant to the Twelve and in his blessing prophesied that he would ever retain possession of his faculties "as long as life lasts." This promise was fulfilled when Elder Anderson died at the age of 102 years.

Elder Joseph Anderson was 80 years of age at the time of his call to serve as an Assistant to the Quorum of the Twelve. Because of his age, he was very surprised to be appointed. Davis Bitton, Assistant Church Historian, recorded the details of how that call came about (Oral Interview, 12 January, 1973). Elder Anderson explained:

I attended all the meetings of the Council of the First Presidency and the Twelve and took minutes of those meetings. Following the Sunday afternoon meeting of General Conference, April 5, 1970, President Lee said to me that I should be there [on April 6th].... I was taking minutes of the meeting and it was there that they announced my appointment. Well, I was greatly surprised, so much so that it was difficult for me to take further notes. President Lee said: "Now, Joseph, if you've got your breath, we would like to hear from you." I can say that I've never before received such a wonderful reception as those brethren gave me; they were just marvelous."

President Harold B. Lee, first counselor in the First Presidency, was voice in setting Elder Joseph Anderson apart as an Assistant to the Quorum of the Twelve. During the course of the blessing President Lee said:

> We bless you with the same health of body which you have heretofore enjoyed in an unusual manner because of the purity of your life and because of your wise keeping of the Word of Wisdom in principle and practice, so that your body is now robust and strong.
>
> We bless you with keenness of mind that you may have possession of all your faculties as long as life lasts, and that your spiritual responses may be enlivened to a degree you have not heretofore enjoyed.

J. Robert Anderson, son of Elder Anderson said that his father "considered this blessing to be very sacred and to be a prophecy of what would occur. He wanted to be certain that he lived up to his responsibility in the prophecy. He therefore did not write of it nor speak of it to others except members of his immediate family."

Elder Anderson retained his faculties as promised right to the end of his life. A week before he passed away, he phoned his son Robert in California where his son was vacationing. "He was anxious for me to return and he asked if I was ready to come home," Robert recalled. "He joked with me many times about my winter vacations in California, and he was bright and clear in his thinking."

When Robert returned the following week, he found his father very ill. Elder Anderson lasted about 48 hours longer. During this last period he called for his mother and two of his brothers many times.

On March 13, 1992, Elder Joseph Anderson died. He was 102 years old. Up to the time of his death, Elder Anderson had retained complete possession of all of his faculties," as long as life last[s]," just as promised by President Lee 22 years earlier.

39

Glen L. Rudd

A Mighty Medical Miracle from God

While paralyzed and not expected to live, a young man is set apart by Apostles for his mission, which he honorably fulfills when completely healed by his priesthood blessings.

Our son Glen Lee, named after President Harold B. Lee, graduated from high school in June of 1961. About that time, he began to suffer from numbness and cold in his hands and feet, and he began to stumble and fall. We took him to our friend, Dr. Rees Anderson, for medical attention. Nevertheless, within two weeks his condition had grown worse. He could not walk.

Again we took him to Dr. Anderson, who engaged Dr. Madison Thomas, a neurologist, for a consultation. Then they immediately admitted Lee to the hospital. We learned that Lee was suffering from an unusual disease known as Guillain-Barre syndrome. Guillain-Barre is similar to polio except that it attacks the nervous system rather than the muscles.

Dr. Anderson told us that Friday afternoon that all of the nerves and muscles of Lee's body were beginning to fail. Lee would need to be hospitalized so that if his breathing became a problem he could be placed in an iron lung. "We know of only two cases like yours," he told us. "Both of them were fatal." He then said bluntly, "Except for a miracle, your boy probably will not make it."

Lee was 18 years of age and was planning to go on a mission

when he turned 19, just six months away.

When I left the doctor's office, I went straight to the Church Administration Building to consult with Elder Harold B. Lee, who had been our family friend and associate for many years. I told Brother Lee the desperate circumstances, and he asked if we had administered to Lee.

I told him we had done so.

"Then he will be all right, at least until Sunday," Elder Lee said. "If you will come to my house Sunday morning, the two of us can go then to the hospital to administer to him."

He didn't tell me what he was going to do, but I knew Brother Lee well enough to know that he wanted to fast and pray and prepare himself to give Lee a special blessing. Brother Lee had told me before this time that he felt as close to my two boys, Lee and Matt, as he did his own grandsons.

When I left his office, I felt better but, of course, was still shaken by the seriousness of our son's condition. I went back to the hospital to join Lee and his mother, who sat at his bedside constantly at that stage. There was a large iron lung sitting in the hall outside of his room on the seventh floor of the hospital, just waiting for emergency action. Lee was unable to talk except in whispers, and he was unable to move any of his limbs or his head. He just lay there and tried desperately to communicate with us.

This was a tremendous crisis in our family. Lee was our eldest son. At a time of his life when he should be experiencing marvelous social and spiritual highlights, he was stricken with this dreaded, potentially fatal disease.

The next morning was Saturday, and I left his hospital room and went down to the lobby. There, by accident, I met President Henry D. Moyle. We visited briefly and then President Moyle asked, "Why are you here?"

"Just visiting someone who is sick," I said evasively.

"Who?" President Moyle pressed. "One of your family?"

For some reason I felt reluctant to talk about our problem, but Elder Moyle made me tell him the circumstances.

He grabbed me by the arm and said, "Let's go up immediately and give that boy a blessing!"

As we entered Lee's room, President Moyle walked over to Lee and looked him straight in the eye. "Lee, I have just talked with your mission president!"

I watched tearfully as our fine son tried desperately to ask a simple question, then I told President Moyle that Lee wanted to know the name of his mission president.

President Moyle told him that his mission president was in New Zealand. He then told Lee that he had come to call him on a mission and to set him apart as a missionary to serve in the New Zealand Mission, the same mission in which I had served. President Moyle then turned to me and said, "Come, let's give him a blessing."

I anointed Lee, and President Moyle sealed the anointing and set him apart as a missionary to serve in the New Zealand Mission, promising him good health and a full and complete recovery from his illness.

At this time Lee was unable to move any part of his body except his eyelids, and the only way he could communicate that he was hearing us was by moving his eyes. We were told by the hospital attendants that everything had ceased to function except the vital organs of his body, and they anticipated that those organs would cease on some time that day. Nevertheless, Lee made it through Saturday.

Early on Sunday morning I called for Brother Lee, and we went to the hospital. There he gave Lee a marvelous blessing and promised him a complete recovery and the restoration of his health. From that moment on, conditions began to markedly improve. Within a day or two, there was no longer any need for the iron lung to be kept a few feet from his bed. Lee responded slowly, but affirmatively, and within a matter of a few weeks we were able to take him home.

After one short relapse, Lee continued to make reasonably good progress. By the end of the summer, he was able to partially use his hands and arms, though still flat on his back and unable to otherwise move. His progress was excellent, except that he had lost the ability to do many of the movements he had learned as a child. He had to learn all over again how to crawl, how to walk, how to button his clothing, tie his shoes and other simple functions of daily care. Though he learned quickly and well, it was a tough time as we tried to help him become more self-sufficient.

My other son, Matthew, and I would carry him into the living room and put him on his hands and knees to give him a chance to try to move from that position. Sometimes he would lay unable to move for 20 minutes, and we would finally have to turn him over bodily because he couldn't move his muscles enough to fall onto his back or onto his side. By his nineteenth birthday in October, we were able to get him out of bed and into a wheelchair for visits in the living room. Soon after that, he was on crutches; and by the time the snow was leaving in February, he was able to walk quite well, even though he did not have good control over his balance.

Lee tried to walk as much as he possibly could to rebuild his leg muscles. He lay in bed for hours lifting dumbbell weights to build up the muscles in his arms. We brushed the last remaining snow aside and arranged for him to bounce a basketball in our backyard. He insisted on doing this by the hour, and after two weeks, he was able to throw the ball up toward the hoop. Gradually he regained his strength and body coordination.

It appeared to everyone, including the physicians, that Lee was going to have a complete recovery from his illness, as had been promised by his priesthood blessings. At this stage he began to ask questions about going on his mission, since he was now four months beyond the time he had planned to leave for the mission field. He began pressing continuously to go. I talked with Elder Lee about it, and we stalled as long as we could. At last the doctors and Elder Lee decided that Lee could plan to leave for his mission in the summer of 1962.

Lee completed a splendid mission and returned home well in

1964, marking the fulfillment of a remarkable prophecy through priesthood blessings. Even today his doctors have only the one explanation—a mighty medical miracle from God.

* * *

It has now been 34 years since Elder Lee blessed our son when he was paralyzed. Lee has led a busy life and has not suffered many effects from the serious illness he had long ago.

Lee graduated from the University of Utah Law School in 1970. Since that time he has practiced his profession in Salt Lake City. He is the father of six children. He has been active in the Church in many capacities, recently completing five years of service on the high council. He has been an excellent son and is very considerate of his parents.

So many, many blessings came from that priesthood administration by President Lee to our son, Lee. President Lee was one of the great men of this dispensation, and I have missed him as much as, or more than, another man since his passing. Many times in my assignments since his death, I have felt close to him.

When I discussed the great men of the Church with President Marion G. Romney, he loved to tell me about the leaders he had known and respected. But when he came to his friend, Harold B. Lee, he always said, "But Harold was a seer."

I know what I have said of President Lee is true, for I remember hundreds of personal moments with him. He was my stake president while I was a young man. We were friends for over 40 years. He treated me like his own son. His greatness has been unmatched in my experience.

40

Elder Marvin J. Ashton

Submitting to God's Will

Sometimes the Lord has a different answer for us. Elder Ashton tells how President Lee couldn't give the blessing he wanted to give.

An unforgettable and frightening experience I once had with President Harold B. Lee was when he invited me to come to his home to participate in giving a blessing to a very sick mutual friend. As we gathered with a few family members President Lee asked me if I would anoint the brother's head with consecrated oil. This I did humbly and in a spirit of inadequacy. I had never before had the opportunity of having this rich spiritual experience of having a Prophet of God seal an anointing that I would pronounce.

I recall with vividness even today President Lee's sealing of this ordinance. It seemed to me he was struggling for words, direction, and guidance to give encouragement to this good brother. I had the feeling he wanted to promise him complete recovery and health from a serious malady, but the words didn't come as he pronounced the sealing. It was evident as the seconds passed he was not only troubled, but groping for direction that would be positive and rewarding, not only to the recipient but to others in the room who had grave concern over the individual's health.

* * *

President Lee never did promise health, strength, and recovery to this individual. He gave words of encouragement and touched on the basics of the total gospel plan, but the promise of healing was not forthcoming.

Immediately following this experience President Lee took me aside in another room and said softly and in perfect mildness, "Marv, he's not going to get better, is he?"

I responded to President Lee, "No. I could tell you wanted to promise this type of blessing, but it was apparently not to be."

I recall his final comment as we walked away from the hearing of family members was, "The Lord has other plans, and he determines not only what we promise but what will happen."

* * *

Many other lessons were taught to me by President Lee. By example he encouraged me and others to be quietly fearless in approaching and solving problems and individual behavior. At the same time he pointed the way for me to show a warmth and tenderness in working with all mankind regardless of where they had been or what they had done. Day after day I learned that President Lee could be firm and totally objective while at the same time he had one of the most tender hearts I have ever witnessed.

President Lee was one of the most spiritual leaders I have ever known. He seemed to have continuous possession of the whisperings of the Spirit. He encouraged me to lead in mildness and quiet patience. He charged me to "seek for that spiritual plus which will add to your natural abilities."

I love that man today as I loved him when I knew him best. He was one of our great leaders and always conveyed the warmth of a special friend. Some of my one-on-one sessions with him are priceless and taught the messages that the whole Church came to love. Everyone wanted to know what he did, what he said, and what his position was on the key issues.

He is still very much a hero to me. His greatness lives on.

Harold B. Lee

Unseen Hands to Bless[1]

On March 27, 1967, as he was returning by airplane from New York City, while very ill, President Lee was twice given priesthood blessings from an unseen personage.

On the occasion of the 143rd General Conference, Sunday, April 8, 1973, President Harold B. Lee related the following:

> Some time ago ... I was suffering from an ulcer condition that was becoming worse and worse. We had been touring a mission [and] my wife, Joan, and I were impressed the next morning that we should get home as quickly as possible, although we had planned to stay for some other meetings.
>
> On the way across the country, we were sitting in the forward section of the airplane. Some of our Church members were in the next section. As we approached a certain point enroute, someone laid his hands upon my head. I looked up; I could see no one. That happened again before we arrived home, again with the same experience. Who it was, by what means or what medium, I may never know, except I knew that I was receiving a blessing that I came a few hours later to know I needed most desperately.
>
> As soon as we arrived home my wife very anxiously called the doctor. It was now about 11 o'clock at night. He called me to come to the telephone, and he asked me how I was. I said,

41

"Well I am very tired; I think I will be all right."

Shortly thereafter, there came massive hemorrhages which, had they occurred while we were in flight, I wouldn't be here today talking about it.

I know that there are powers divine that reach out when all other help is not available. We see that manifest down in the countries we speak of as the underprivileged countries where there is little medical aid and perhaps no hospitals. If you want to hear of great miracles among these humble people with simple faith, you will see it among them when they are left to themselves.

Yes, I know that there are such powers.

Notes

[1]President Harold B. Lee, taken from the *Ensign*, May 1974, p. 16. (See also the 143rd General Conference Report, Sunday, 8 April 1973, p. 179.)

42

President Gordon B. Hinckley

A Mighty Miracle in a Land of Miracles

I now realize I was skirting on the brink of eternity and a miracle, in this land of ever great miracles, was extended by a merciful God who obviously was prolonging my ministry for a longer time, to give to him in whose service I am, all the strength of my heart, mind, and soul....—H.B.L.

I shall always be grateful for the opportunity that was mine, with my wife, Marjorie, to be with President and Sister Harold B. Lee when we traveled together in the British Isles and in Israel in September of 1972. I can never forget the night he was sick in the Intercontinental Hotel in Jerusalem.

According to my dictated journal I recorded throughout our tour, we met at the Garden Tomb on September 20, 1972, with the Saints who lived in Israel. They were few in number, about 30 persons including young children. It was a most inspirational and wonderful experience.

As we stood in the tomb cut from stone, we could imagine Joseph of Arimathea, Mary, and others bringing the body of Jesus and laying it there in a hurry to have this done before the Jewish Sabbath. We could then imagine the first day of the week, when the burial clothes were left in the tomb, but the body was gone, the stone being rolled away. We could imagine the two angels sitting at either end of the tomb, and Peter and others of the Apostles coming and looking in consternation at the empty burial place. And then we could see in our mind's eye the risen Lord with Mary, and hear again the conversation which took place.

It seemed to us that this was in very deed the place of the burial and resurrection of the Master, the place where occurred the greatest event in human history, when the Master of Life broke the bands of death.

We sang "We Thank Thee, Oh God, for a Prophet." Prayer was offered by Brother Tvedtnes, first counselor in the branch presidency. Brother David Brian Galbraith was sustained as President of the Jerusalem Branch of the Church (the first branch of the Church to be organized in the Holy Land in nearly 2,000 years). He then spoke, followed by Mission President Edwin Q. Cannon, Jr. A new convert then played and sang one of the psalms. I then spoke, recounting from the Book of John some of the events of the death, burial, and resurrection of the Savior and bore testimony of his living reality, the Son of God, the Savior and Redeemer of Mankind. A group of small children then sang "I Am a Child of God."

President Harold B. Lee then spoke. He said that when he and his wife came to the Garden Tomb in 1958 there was a feeling about this place that was different from all other places. He read the scripture, "In the place where he was crucified there was a garden." He concluded that Golgotha was right up on the top of the hill above here and that this was indeed the very garden where Joseph of Arimathea brought the body of the crucified Lord.

President Lee told the group assembled, "Though you are few in number, you are laying the foundation of something that will be great." He indicated that in the visits we had made to various officials during the day, there had been a respect expressed for us greater than we could hope. He went on to say, "When people ask you who you are, don't say 'members of the Mormon Church,' nor of the LDS, say 'The Church of Jesus Christ of Latter-day Saints.'" He then bore a powerful and moving testimony of the Savior.

We sang "Now Let Us Rejoice," after which Brother Brandly offered prayer. We set apart Brother Galbraith and Brother Tvedtnes and then we sang "God Be with You Til We Meet Again." No one present will ever forget this occasion.

The fast and long pace of the day had fatigued President Lee, whose body was weakened by his chronic lung disease. I later learned that back at the hotel this night President Lee wrote in his journal of his concern over his physical condition and pain:

> These are exhausting days. My physical strength is at a seriously low ebb. I know something is seriously wrong. There is a severe pain in my lower back and a weariness that was emphasized by a constant effort to expel mucus. Joan insisted that I have Brother Hinckley and President Cannon administer to me.

When we were about to retire Sister Lee knocked on my door and asked if we would give President Lee a blessing. President Cannon anointed him and I sealed the anointing. I felt the power of the Spirit of the Lord and as I invoked the blessing I rebuked the Destroyer. I felt confident that the Lord would heal His servant.

President Lee appeared stronger the next morning, but said only that he felt better. When we had finished breakfast two days after the blessing, President Lee shared with us his testimony that the Lord had brought to pass a miracle in his behalf in response to the blessing given him. His health was remarkably improved, for which we were grateful. The President said, "We had to come to the land of miracles to witness a miracle within ourselves."

The journal entry by President Lee, published later in his biography, reveals the fulfillment of the blessing and the miracle:

> The next morning, after a severe coughing spell, I expelled two clots which seemed to be blood—one, about the size of a dime, was like dried blood, and the other one was red, as a

fresh clot. Immediately my shortness of breath ceased, the weariness was diminished, and the back pains began to subside, and 24 hours later they were entirely gone.

I now realize I was skirting on the brink of eternity and a miracle, in this land of ever great miracles, was extended by a merciful God who obviously was prolonging my ministry for a longer time, to give to him in whose service I am, all the strength of my heart, mind, and soul, to indicate in some measure my gratitude for his never-failing consideration to me and my loved ones.

Undoubtedly the expelled material had nearly blocked off one of the lobes in his lungs. Divine intervention had rescued him from a most serious extremity; he died 15 months later.

President Harold B. Lee was a great light in my life. I had many happy associations with him. Notable among them were the two occasions when we traveled together in Europe.

The Holy Land miracle will be always remembered with gratitude.

Epilogue: Hosanna Moments[1]

Richard M. Cracroft

Many of you know what I am talking about when I speak of "Hosanna Moments," those transcendent moments in our lives when, without warning, we are overwhelmed by a Close Encounter with Eternity, a Surprise of the Spirit—those moments, when, while engaged in the temporal rhythms of our daily and earth-encrusted lives, comfortably duped by familiar routines, we are suddenly brought face-to-face with the Holy, swept by the Spirit of God into a transcendent reality, overwhelmed by the undeniable evidence of a literal Father in Heaven who knows you and knows me, and is somehow interested and involved in our lives. The "We'll Sing and We'll Shout Moment" is that moment when our God, Brother of Jared-ing us, reaches His hand through the veil to startle our sensibilities, to reassure, to comfort, to guide, to prod, to change our course. Our spirits soar, our souls are renewed, and we can never really be the same again.

It is my experience that, in one way or another, these glimpses of Eternity come to most of us. Nudging us toward our destiny, His welcome and too-infrequent interventions shout to our souls that our Heavenly Father lives! That His purpose is "to bring to pass [our] immortality and eternal life" (Moses 1:39); that we "live our lives in the eye of the Father, ... not at the periphery but at the center of his vision" (Dr. Scott Peck); and that our "God is everywhere present," Brigham Young told us, "by the power of His Spirit—His minister, the Holy Ghost."

Most Latter-day Saints, upon hearing [a miracle story], will generally feel—depending on their spiritual equilibrium at the moment—the familiar thrill of spiritual recognition (you know what I mean—the shiver through the body, the cold chill across the back, the flash across spirit, and yes, the burning in the bosom), and he will nod his head affirmatively, or she will smile her knowing smile, and adding the new testimony to their stories of such testimonies, they will ask if you have a moment to listen to an experience which just recently occurred in their lives—and, behold, we're enjoying an impromptu testimony meeting.

The Holy Spirit shall come to you, this afternoon, tomorrow, or the day after. And when He comes, be grateful, honor His presence, heed His admonitions, and He shall abide with you. And then "shall thy confidence wax strong in the presence of God; and the doctrine of the priesthood shall distill upon thy soul as the dews from heaven. The Holy Ghost shall be thy constant companion ... forever and ever." (D&C 121:45-46)

Notes

[1]Richard M. Cracroft, excerpts from a devotional address given at Brigham Young University, Provo, Utah, on 29 June 1993.

ABOUT THE AUTHOR

L. Brent Goates was born and raised in Salt Lake City. He has worked as administrator of the LDS Hospital in Salt Lake City and assistant commissioner for the Church's multihospital system, Health Services Corporation. He has also served as director of missionary operations in the Church's Missionary Department.

Brother Goates has served in such Church positions as bishop, stake president, mission president, and Regional Representative. He is the author of two previous books: *Harold B. Lee: Prophet and Seer* and *He Changed My Life: Personal Experiences with Harold B. Lee.*

Brother Goates is married to Helen Lee, President Harold B. Lee's daughter, and the couple have six children.